CHASING
THE KINGDOM

Turning: The Experience of Conversion

Clinging: The Experience of Prayer

Pope John Paul II Visits the City of New Orleans
(with William Griffin)

CHASING THE KINGDOM

A Parable of Faith

EMILIE GRIFFIN

1817

Harper & Row, Publishers, San Francisco

New York, Grand Rapids, Philadelphia, St. Louis
London, Singapore, Sydney, Tokyo, Toronto

Grateful acknowledgement is made for permission to reprint "Why weep and slumber": lyrics from "Every Man a King," words and music by Huey P. Long and Castro Carazo. Reprinted with permission of Louisiana and Lower Mississippi Valley Collections, LSU Libraries, Baton Rouge, LA. Originally published by National Book Co., 1935.

FIRST EDITION

Library of Congress Cataloging-in-Publication Data

Griffin, Emilie.
  Chasing the kingdom: a parable of faith, Emilie Griffin—1st ed.
  p. cm.

   ISBN 0–06–063466–9
   1. Parables. 2. Christian life—1960– I. Title.
BV4515.2.G74 1990
248.2—dc20   89–45556
                                    CIP

90 91 92 93 94 HAD 10 9 8 7 6 5 4 3 2 1

FOR WILLIAM

Servant of the Rightful King

The persons and places in this book are
imaginary.
While some references to States of the Union
are included, the country intended is entirely
mythical.
The author wishes, by means of characters
and landscapes, to depict
the terrain of the heart.

The Kingdom goes before us as we labor. The least small flower says, "Forget me not."
We climb in hopes of Horeb and of Tabor
Thinking beyond each rise lies Camelot.
Smiling at grief, flinty to others' laughter,
Seizing alike the roses and the thorns;
Living each valley for what may come after,
Holding our breath to hear the silver horns.
You were my guide who parted every bramble;
Cutting our path, you saw more plain than I.
Yet each is entered on a matchless gamble,
Caught in our humanness until we die.
Christ only goes before, and in new guise
Teases and hints to lead us to the prize.

Contents

CHASING
THE KINGDOM

CHAPTER ONE

Chasing

———◆————

In which the Author explains
the true nature of her journey.

Now a traveler must make her way to Resurrection City by the best means she can, for there are no buses or trains heading in that direction.

She would be well-advised to have a guide, one who has a good sense of the terrain, for the way is hard and often puzzling.

The true path lies through a zone of unknowing, across peaks of insight and valleys of doubt. From time to time it will be necessary to make a leap of thought or to cross a bridge of metaphor. There are great Quandaries to be met, Monsters of Unknown Origin, welling up from the depths of the soul; one must cross through landscapes where the compass entirely fails and go on by faith and judgment, without any clear sense of what lies ahead. Also, though fleeting, there will be unexpected stings of joy, cloudbursts of blessing, sunbursts of happiness. Nothing can be fully predicted or anticipated. Only now and then is there a vision of the city or perhaps something that promises such a city may exist. But the road is unmarked, and great courage will be needed.

The traveler is ourselves, our collective aspiration, our joint longing for justice—all the levels of soul and spirit warring within us, yearning for peace. It is she who takes us on a wilderness journey to find the lost city of comfort and resolution.

This She-Child is our spirit of contemplation, the creative and mystical self, which smooths rough-hewn reality till it pleases her, till it matches some inner vision of her own.

Her vision is not only hers but also ours. We were told it of old. We heard it on our mother's lap; it is like a lullaby—so old we can barely remember.

We are covenant people. We are going somewhere. As travelers we are bound together with hoops of steel, tied with cords of friendship. We are coming from a thousand places, with a thousand stories to tell. But the burning in our hearts is the same burning.

"Were not our hearts burning within us on the road?"

We are on the way to Emmaus, chasing the Kingdom. We are on the road to Damascus, chasing the Kingdom.

We are lost, we are afraid, we are frightened. We have been in this wilderness for forty years, and we have nothing to eat. We have listened to Moses and Aaron; we have heard their grandiose and crazy promises, and we are not sure we want to be people of the promise any more.

But we know there is a true king, and he will not abandon us. He is the anointed one, in exile, and we will restore him. We will rise up against the kings of earth, the false prophets who mislead and betray. We will tell them we are following another king and looking for his Kingdom.

He was with us once, and we remember him. We know very nearly the day of his birth, and we know the place of it. We know who his parents are, his mother and father. We know the places he lived and taught, in villages by the sea.

We know the healings he did, those he ate and drank with, those he raised from death. We know the promises he made. And he is faithful. He has chosen us to be his people, and we are faithful to him.

We have come a long way, yet the story up to now is fragmentary. Our scholars and historians have written things down. They have told us how it was of old—how the meal was made into cakes, how the oil was poured, what it meant to be a young woman and betrothed. We tell the stories again and again to remember him. We want to understand the one we are following, the story we are part of. We want to know who he is and who we are. So we remember as well as we can the things he told us. "Can you drink this cup that I drink of? Can you walk this road that I walk? Can you give yourself as I give myself? Can you travel with me all the way to the end?"

He speaks to us softly, yet his words burn in our hearts. It is not a scolding, yet his words demand more of us; they haunt us with a sense that more is possible, that we have more to give and more to do. "What description can I find for this generation? We played the pipes for you, and you wouldn't dance; we sang dirges, and you wouldn't be mourners. . . . And still, I tell you that it will not go as hard with the land of Sodom on Judgment Day as with you."

Is it time now to listen to this powerful, persistent call? To this voice from the heights of creation and from the depths of the heart?

Is it time to admit we have failed? That we have been lackluster and lukewarm? Is it time to set off again with just a few crusts of bread tied in a napkin and trust the Lord to provide bread for the journey? Is it time to set aside our disenchantment and start believing again that dreams come true?

This is the way the path leads, with clues scattered at random. Always the She-Child leads us. In the next chapter I will name her. But named or nameless, she is the inner prompting that calls us to our destiny, the longing that moves us to chase the Kingdom.

And you, gentle reader, will find your spiritual profit in this little book as it leads you through a geography that has no map. You must walk spiritually through a maze of problems and figures, up, down, this way and that, now in stillness and contemplation, sometimes called to strive and persevere, holding still, then falling into *the abyss*, passing over, passing through, on a search for your real being and your heart's desire.

Give way to it all and listen to the inner voice, the child in you who speaks and leads, who scampers and plays. Listen to the Lord calling you deeper into the mystery of himself.

Each chapter is a hint of the Kingdom, a clue to holiness and justice. You will hear yourself speaking or find yourself in the child with many royal names. You will see angels and be led by them. You will fall down rabbit holes and enter the garden of prayer. As the journey continues, it is my hope that you will see the Person you are chasing, the Kingdom you are living for. You will confront the great Quandaries, Monsters and Riddles; the Incompleteness of Things as They Are; you will discover the many companions who are traveling the road with you.

I beg you not to read this book but to eat it, so that you may enter by a mystery into the pathways of the Lord in search of the city that is both now and later, the Kingdom that has come and is to come.

CHAPTER TWO
The Riddle of Existence

In which travelers
are discovered whose ringleader
is a Lady-Child.

When the travelers got to the edge of existence, they stopped and tried to puzzle out what was going on.

"It's impossible," said the Child. "There must be something more to existence than this. Is that all there is to it?"

The Child was named Lady Zane. It was her own personal choice of name, picked from the many names her family had given her. Like a royal child, she had quite a few: Dorothy Alice Mary Zane Melanie Storey. But none of those other names suited her half as well as Zane, which reminded her of Wild West adventures. The addition of Lady gave her just the right amount of authority and panache, allowing her to hold sway over fellow pilgrims who were older and, in some instances, taller than she: Nasja-the-Good, a Piute guide, who was good at negotiating mountain passes; Ol' Will

Smoky, the Cowpoke, who was skilled at breaking broncos and riding the purple sage; and the cowardly Cougar, or Mountain Lion, named Slim; not to mention Zane's small dog Rover, who rode comfortably along with her in a basket, except sometimes when he excitedly jumped out, usually during appearances of angels or when feeling the rumbles of earthquakes and temblors.

Lady Zane was the smartest. It was principally by the force of her intelligence that she managed to retain her slender command. For the group was decidedly raggle-taggle and hardly could be kept together except by means of some imaginative, resourceful leadership. This came naturally to Lady Zane, however. The others liked her for her spirit of adventure, her willingness to try new things. Each member of the group had his or her own role to play, as everyone understood. In fact, one would almost have thought they all were really one person with moods of cowboyhood, Piutehood, lionhood, and even frisky Roverhood.

Now, however, the little group was baffled and exhausted. They were disappointed to think they had come through so many trials and adventures and there was nothing to look forward to but a wall.

In fact, it was hardly a proper wall. It was much more like a question mark, an empty space. There was nothing sharply divided, nothing you could really put your finger on, nothing as concrete as existence having an end. There was nothing particular in front of them. They did not know how the next step could be taken or even where a destination could be.

"I'm afraid," said the Mountain Lion.

"Don't add up," said the Cowpoke.

"It doesn't seem fair that we've come all this way only to find ourselves stranded at this point," said the Piute, who had studied philosophy at Berkeley and was concerned about justice issues.

But Lady Zane was sure there must be more to existence than the blank space ahead. She sat down and thought for a while.

"I know," she said at last. "It's a riddle. The Riddle of Existence."

"Oh, that explains everything," said the rest, somewhat sarcastically.

Reader, let me explain. The Riddle of Existence can be simply stated in two questions: "What is it?" and "Where can I find it?" Questions that you will immediately recognize if you have ever thought about anything. Such questions are with us from earliest memory. We hardly remember a time when we failed to ask them. No matter how often we lay them to rest, with interim, pacifying answers, the questions jump up again, needling us, demanding to be dealt with. When she encountered the riddle, Lady Zane began to think hard about what it was and how she might respond to it. Her thoughts followed this vein:

First, she thought about It—the relentless It our whole being yearns for but cannot fully grasp or know. She saw It there, just ahead, dancing.

She recognized It—the lure of what-is-not-yet and what-could-yet-be. It—that merciless vision of possibilities; that terrifying glimpse of freedom; that haunting glimmer of experience not yet tasted, vintages unsipped; that stretch of blue we prisoners call the sky; that something beyond, that powerful something, which is painful and compelling.

There ahead, just beyond, mingling with the horizon yet not defined by any horizon line, something summons and baffles us, something we have to follow.

Then Lady Zane saw a blank space. She knew It was hiding again. Just when she thought she could see It plainly, riding like the night moon through the trees, then the road seemed to twist, the space went blank, the vision was gone. "I am alone," she thought. "I am terrified. The dream I was dreaming has been interrupted. The screen is dark, the computer is out of repair."

"Where is It? And can any Being that is all power forget, even for a moment, to be? Is there some defect of vision that makes the Great It go out of sight now and then? Is there any escape, or is a person caught in this dance forever?"

All this might seem a bit complicated for a mere slip of a child like Lady Zane, but she had simply drifted into one of her customary reveries, as you might do if you were up against the Riddle of Existence.

"I am small," she reflected, "but I battle against enormous odds. I am brave in that I go in search of what is greater than I. I am adventurous; I summon up all my courage. I run, I dance, I chase! I hurl myself into the center of experience, and I weigh a riddle inside myself; then holding it at arm's length, I reckon the size of the riddle as well as I can. I put a tape measure to my bafflement. I don't ask much. Only to know who I am, who made me, what I was created for. I want to chase my destiny, to run after my star. What I am chasing is not within me but beyond me. I hurry to know not just myself but Whatever Is, Whatever Acts. I rush to follow the star that calls me; I race to the white-hot center of existence that says, 'Draw near.'

"I will not be satisfied with half-answers and part-truths, with children's stories, unless they are true stories. I will not settle for dim and dreary substitutes for life. I want experience. To capture existence, I will run, I will follow, I will chase the dream.

"I will not yield to discouragement. I will not give way to disillusionment. I will sweep disenchantment aside with a wave of my hand. I will believe, always, in the possibility of newness, the creative advance into novelty. I will affirm that existence is going somewhere.

"I will see Good, burning like gold, in the center of everything. I will run from the murderous ax of the wicked queen into the forest where the good dwarves and fairies can hide me. I will chase the Kingdom. I will capture the dream.

"I will enter into childhood again. I will find the door. I will stoop down and enter in where only the little ones can enter. I will make friends with the trolls and the little people of earth, the earthkins; I will become one of them. I will let my feet grow furry as the Hobbit's. I will grow young again in the best way, by becoming very simple and small.

"I will look up at the tops of the mushrooms and walk among the high arching blades of summer grass, and there I will see It. My Love, my Answer, my Beloved, my Fulfillment, peering at me through the stalks and saying, "I am here, come find me."

Having followed this train of thought for some time, Lady Zane got up and said, "I know what we must do. We'll create something."

"What sort of thing," said the others.

"This is the answer," said Lady Zane. "We have come to the end of what presently exists, and we can only make headway into something new by creating it."

"But that's absurd. We're only creatures," said Cougar.

"How can we create something," Nasja wondered, "when God has already created everything?"

"It's part of the game," she explained. "He wants us to create things."

"So that we can become more like him?" said Cowpoke.

"I think so. I'm not sure about that."

"Well, what are you sure of?"

"The creative advance into novelty. It's a philosophical idea, but it's also about the way things really are."

"I still don't understand."

"When you come to the edge of existence, you find a riddle. And the riddle is a blank space. And when you find yourself at the blank space, you create something to go into it, and you move deeper into existence."

"By faith? By prayer? By pretending? By believing?"

"I don't know how you do it. You just do it. By chasing. It's so much fun, it's easy; you don't think about it, you simply do it."

"I'm tired," said Slim the Cougar.

"I don't feel creative," said the Cowpoke.

"We've come all this way, through dark forests and over the roots of trees," said the Piute, "figuring out which way is north from the bark on one side of the trees, and now you're telling us to create something?"

"It's the only way out," Zane said.

"What do you mean, the only way out?"

"We can always go back where we came from."

"And where was that?" Lady Zane wanted to know.

"Why, we came from . . . over there, I think . . . that way . . . no, that way," said the Cougar; he had a natural sense of direction, but in this foreign place it failed him.

Now they understood: it was getting hard to remember. They knew they had some beginnings; it had taken them a long time to get this far, to set out on an expedition into existence, a brand-new sort of exploit, but they had kept no log of it. There was no way to reconstruct what had gone before.

"Very well, if you're so stubborn, I'll go first, and then you'll see how simple it is," said Lady Zane; then she moved into the blank space, and the others went with her and something new occurred.

Precisely at the intersection between God and the travelers, the Riddle of Existence was posed and answered, and the chase was able to continue for a little while longer.

CHAPTER THREE

A Sea of Troubles

In which Lady Zane and her companions
are frightened by nameless monsters
and find a protector.

After a while the travelers noticed the ground had slipped away. They had cut loose from their moorings. They were adrift, not making for a clear destination, but awash in a Sea of Troubles.

No doubt of it, there were monsters close by. And they had no way to name them. All very well if they were the four dragons of legendary fame. On the contrary, these monsters were shapeless and nameless. They were hovering in the dark and came out of their caves only to roar, from time to time, and to loll at the edge of the sea. These are the monsters who seize us daily by the throat and drive us quietly mad. They are the ones that poison our daily lives, Monsters of Confusion and Despair.

Who could slay these monsters? Who could stand in the place of God, raising his shield and buckler?

A SEA OF TROUBLES

Holy Michael Archangel, defend us in battle.
Be our protection against the wickedness
and snares of the Devil;
Rebuke him, we humbly pray.
And by the power of the Holy Spirit, cast
into hell Satan and all the other spirits who
roam the world, seeking the ruin of souls.

Then on the edge of the Sea of Troubles, mounted on a white steed, the children saw him. His face was blazing with light; his garment was dazzling. He stood in the stirrups, seeming too large to be a man, mastering the moment.

Lady Zane and her companions were in awe. "Who are you then, wearing those shining garments?"

"Fear not, children," the answer came. "I am Michael, and I will be your guide on the journey."

For it is written, "He shall give his angels charge over you, to keep you in all your ways. I will bear you up in my hands, lest you dash your foot against a stone."

Then they looked, and under his lance they saw the body of a writhing monster, and its form was satanic. The hot fire of its breathing lashed up toward the belly of the angel's mount; the ugly thing twisted on the sand as Michael thrust his lance. The pilgrims hid their eyes, for it was hideous.

But Michael said, "You must look, for it is not given to the children of the Kingdom to forget the presence of evil. You must be on guard against it everywhere and in every way."

And behind him the ocean roared and lashed, and the great spray of it bathed his face and the sound of the waters was mighty and dreadful.

And Michael said again, "You shall not be afraid of the terror by night nor of the arrow that flies by day. Nor of the pestilence that walks in darkness, nor the destruction that lays waste at noonday."

When Lady Zane and the other travelers saw that the dragon had been killed and that Michael was victorious over the wicked spirits, they were quietly grateful for a little while.

Presently Lady Zane made up a little verse and scribbled it in her notebook. Her writing was filled with erasures and crossings out, but at last she was satisfied.

At first she was too shy to recite the verse to the Angel. So bright was he, so exalted, it seemed hard to approach him as a friend. Finally, she took a deep breath and said, "Might I read you the poem? It is the only way I know to express my gratitude."

Then one of the other pilgrims made a noise like the sound of a rejoicing tambourine. And Lady Zane said:

Michael before God
shining,

your foot is on the dragon's
throat.
Your prayer
scatters wicked things that
lurk
in darkness.
Goodness in you
glints like a sword,
catching sunlight
in God's service.
He delights in you
as I do.
He has appointed me
lady and messenger
to tell you of his love.

Then Michael said, "You hold me too much in awe, Lady Zane, for I am a creature like yourself. Remember that you, too, have power over the evil spirits. For it is not my power but the Lord's that destroys wickedness and casts out demons. To slay the monsters who strangle us, you must name them and ask the Lord's power over them. Call them by name: You, Anxiety! You, Fear! You, Trembling! You, Despair! Name them and make them subject to you. They will subside; they will vanish like mist. And the Lord's peace be with you."

"And also with you."

"Lift up your hearts."

"We lift them up to the Lord."

In time, the Angel was gone, and a great light remained that bathed the pilgrims in a pool of holiness. And they were content and eager to continue the journey.

CHAPTER FOUR

Where the Compass Fails

In which the Author,
calling herself "we,"
explains spiritual geography,
with some help
from a twelfth-century mystic.

Shall I go with you
into a zone
beyond the commonsensical
where place is meaningless
and zero is everything?

the region of blind nought,
where to enter
is possible

only when the bridge of reason
crumbles
and certainty becomes laughable?

Do I dare to cut the strings
of supposition,
strangle the infant Hypothesis
in his cradle
and, by some scrambling of the codes
that bind us,
undecipher

the mystery of things?

As if it were possible
to know
knowing
and by experiment find
an insight into mind.

To cross that unknown distance,
which is both absolute beyond
and at the same time
intimately near,

And will you be for me
Charon, Vergil, and the Pied Piper
all at once,

running before me
into a mountainside
that did not loom till now?
Rising one day in a century
out of the mist
until we enter
and disappear

on the other side of the chasm,
Time?

Lethe is flowing
underneath my feet.
And when I cross that river of
forgetting,
I do not know what I will know.
Yet I will follow,
even so.

What lies beyond us is a plunge into a new dimension of experience.

"Lord, we do not know where you are going, so how can we know the way?"

Have you noticed, across the river and through the trees, how the road winds and twists? The destination is hidden from our sight, but there is no mistaking the road. We have only to follow it, and somehow we will be at Jerusalem.

But we've noticed one thing. In this uncharted country of ours, there is a rule, an order, a ruler, a kingdom.

How do we know it? We who have never lived in any earthly kingdom? Still, we recognize the spiritual kingdom—even if it was just a metaphor in the first place!

Some memory of a lost reign stays with us and reminds us: there is an inner realm, a kingdom in our hearts, Jesus said the reign of God is within us.

It is a country that you enter, not by going somewhere but by going nowhere, not by conquest but by surrender. There is no sense in being Cortez. No need for a show of steel and military might. It is a country of peace and a kind of inexpressible wonder. You will know you are there when the compass fails.

The Way into Nowhere is like this. You are traveling on foot through wild country with your compass in your hand. You have all your trusty boy scout and girl scout know-how about ways to build a fire, how to pitch a tent, where to make camp. You have the most reliable device in history, a compass. It tells you one way is north; the other, south; east and west are opposites. You're well oriented. The sun won't surprise you by coming up on the wrong side of your sleeping bag.

Now you can forget all that. We're setting our course for unknown country, where the needle starts to spin. No, it's not the Arctic Circle. This time, you're in a place that didn't exist before. You created it, God and you. It's the inner space in which you meet, your confrontation, your encounter—where everything is brand new.

Our God is the Lord of Surprises, who calls us over the Rim of the World, beyond the known into the unknown. He has promised to be with us there, where the compass fails.

Is it possible, when entering Nowhere, to imagine where we are? Look, our little ship is setting a straight course for Zero. We're going to slip right through it. Look your last on images, for in Nowhere we won't need them!

But to this you say: "Where then shall I be? By your reckoning I am to be nowhere!"

Exactly. In fact, you have expressed it rather well, for I would indeed have you be nowhere" . . .

Nowhere physically. Everywhere spiritually.

Go on with this nothing, moved only by your love for the Lord.

Never give up, but steadfastly persevere in this nothing, consciously longing that you may always choose to possess God through love, whom no one can possess through knowledge.

For myself, I prefer to be lost in this nowhere, wrestling with this blind nothingness, than to be like some great lord travelling everywhere. . . .

Everywhere . . . pales in richness beside this blessed nothingness and nowhere.

Don't worry if your faculties fail to grasp it.

For this nothingness is so lofty that they cannot reach it.

It cannot be explained, only experienced.

Nowhere. What a blessed kingdom, where the compass fails. Maybe we could coin a word and call it New-where. Because in this Nowhere, something new occurs. Something happens for the first time between the Lord and us. Some spark jumps from his divinity to our humanity, something beyond our power to capture or explain.

It is a new creation, this spark leaping from God to us and back again to God. New-where. New-when. Perhaps even New-what. Something so original that it never happened quite this way before. Yet we know it was prepared for us from the foundation of the world.

It is like that expression of Whitehead's—the creative advance into novelty. Whitehead's phrase reminds us of the daring advance of prayer, the dance of prayer. We make advances to the Lord because of all the advances he made to us. And in the minuet of existence, some new steps are invented. Whitehead says God is creating the world new again; with every step, every action, creation advances into novelty. We experience this. We validate that hypothesis when we pray.

But, then, possibly, the Bible anticipates Whitehead: "See, I am doing a new deed, even now it comes to light."

Even then, creation was open-ended. It's a fair supposition that the Hebrews didn't know about Nowhere. Zero is an arabic numeral, and nought hadn't been conceived of yet. Not to mention minus one.

Infinity came later. Before it was found, did it exist? Infinity, where parallel lines converge, where opposites make friends.

But maybe the Hebrews had some inkling, some messianic hints:

> The wolf lives with the lamb,
> the panther lies down with the kid,
> calf and lion cub feed together
> with a little boy to lead them.
> The cow and the bear make friends

their young lie down together.
The lion eats straw like the ox.
The infant plays over the cobra's hole;
into the viper's lair the young child puts his hand.
They shall do no hurt, no harm
on all my holy mountain,
for the country is filled with the knowledge of
Yahweh
as the waters swell the sea.

CHAPTER FIVE

Holding Still

In which the Prayerful Self,
learning the practice of humility,
is transformed into various
lowly creatures, just as young
Arthur was once schooled
by Merlin for his kingly call.

If I stay here in the tall grass (says the self at prayer), they will not be able to find me. I am well hidden now. They may call me from the house and say it is bath time, but if I am in the tall grass I need not go. I am hidden here, and I can be anyplace, anyone, anywhere. I am with the Lord. I am invisible. I am safe.

The more I am with the Lord, holding still, the smaller I can become. I can snuggle into the furry petals of a nasturtium. I am able to jump up onto the stalk of a zinnia and climb over the petals, one by one. The zinnia is thick with sticky petals. Something like an aster or a daisy. I am in heaven. I am home.

It is hard to decide whether I prefer to be an elf or a rabbit—I just want to be some congenial garden creature who doesn't have to go in for a bath. Garden creatures don't have lessons. They don't have to do grown-up things. They never have to balance their checkbooks or take the car to the shop. When I am in the garden with the Lord of the Garden, I am a child again. I am free from the cares and concerns of daily life. I am holding still.

And when a bird flies into the garden, I can hold my breath. I can inch closer and closer and listen to the warble of her song. I can watch the cardinals cluster on the branch, holding a college council. They are electing a feathery pope perhaps. At any rate they are robed in splendor because my heavenly father feeds them.

When I am in the garden with my Lord, I am all creatures. I can take flight with the mockingbirds and do satirical impressions on the highest branch. I can stalk with the curvy, stealthy cat who wants to run the robins down. I can slither with the lizard and show the red throat of my distinction, giving glory to God by my existence. I can creep with the caterpillar, loving my fuzziness, not in any hurry to be somewhere. I can jump with the squirrel.

I can even be a leaf! Now I am truly still. Only the raindrops, splashing, drenching me, can disturb my concentration. Only the hot bucketfuls of the sun can wilt me now and then. But always I am at peace.

I am holding still, with the birds of the air and the fish of the sea and the lilies of the field. I toil not, I spin not, yet Solomon in all his glory was never dressed like me!

Thank you, precious Merlin, for teaching me my lessons well. Teaching me how to hold still as creatures born to kingship must do, how to enter into the life of the world, how to be others than I—even the littlest others, powerless under the sky.

Now I am Arthur elfkin, and I scamper from leaf to leaf, snuggling under the earth because I am a worm at last. I know, in prayer, how powerless I am. And I slither, warmly, gratefully, thoughtlessly, through the mire, with eyes that cannot see the stars. Nevertheless, you are with me. Your power is round about me. The God who made the stars and flung the planets made me, too—even I, Worm—and I wend my way through the wonder of the garden, praising you. Gladly, joyfully, shouting the Worm's Worship Song, glad to live only as long as you will it, O Thou Lovely Ancient of Days.

> Where the bee sucks, there suck I,
> In a cowslip's bell I lie,
> There I couch when owls do cry.
> On the bat's back I do fly
> After summer merrily.

HOLDING STILL

Merrily, merrily shall I live now
Under the blossom that hangs on the bough.

CHAPTER SIX

Down the Rabbit Hole

In which the Pilgrim Self experiences
the free fall of the abyss
and makes some surprising discoveries.

Oh, my God, now I'm in for it. They've
gone and made me a rabbit and me not
having the slightest thing to say about it. Or was it
that little bottle on the table that said "Drink me?"
I do believe the Lord is playing tricks. I'm not a
rabbit at all. I'm still a child, and I'm falling, falling,
falling, like that stewardess in James Dickey's poem,
the one who fell out of the plane, falling forever,
through the wind, through the stratosphere,
through the atmosphere, down to the land of the
underworld, down to the bottom of the universe,
where no man or woman has yet traveled, into the
abyss.

I am falling, says the Pilgrim Self as it plummets
into the abyss. There is nothing, no one under me,
and the world has no floor. There is nothing under
earth or heaven to break my fall. Only God can
rescue me. And I am afraid.

I am afraid because there is no end in sight, and the darkness is covering me, because there is no security anywhere, no place to hold on, no chance to cling.

I am down the rabbit hole in a place from which there is no returning, and in this dark descent, there is no certainty, no assurance, no consolation, no place to run.

But look, as I fall through the dark tunnel into the abyss, I see, on this side and that, there are rooms, little rooms in the wall of my despair that show me glimpses of reality. A person having a tea party and using a cup and saucer. Yes, even while the world is being utterly destroyed, still it is possible to use a cup and saucer.

Look, over there, I see a person sweeping up and washing dishes. We are under the earth, far down, near the gates of hell, I am quite sure, and yet there is a person sweeping up and washing dishes.

I am descending, there is no bottom, no place to stand, yet there is on the other side of me an old man, climbing precariously up the library steps and blowing dust from the covers of the oldest books in the world.

There on the other side are beavers, having breakfast *en famille,* flashing those beavery smiles at each other as though it were simply another day of the week. Look, on the other side there are Royal

Mice dressed in their palace attire, with velvet jackets and fluttery pinafores, peering at me through their spectacles and bowing gracefully before they begin to dance.

How can I be afraid, even in this constantly falling state, in this bottomless pit where no sanity remains, since there are little glimpses of Your Presence here, along the dark and totally invisible rabbit-hole walls? If they be walls.

I am in prison. I am hospitalized. The straitjacket I wear is the badge of my effort to make sense out of existence when existence makes no sense at all. The questions I raise are the right questions, those questions that must be shouted to the orderlies who make no answer, namely: "How long will you hold me prisoner here? Who is in charge? Do I have a right to an attorney? When will there be a trial? In the event that there is a firing squad, will it be humane? Is there justice in this place? If so, who can I take up my case with? When and how will we put things right?" But the questions ring hollow as I fall, century by century, through the madness of existence. And there is no place to stand. There is not even a railing to catch on to; the sides of the walls are slippery, and surely Satan is nearby.

But You are there. With Your right hand, You hold me. Even so, the holding is a faith holding, not an interruption of my descent.

My descent into madness is reality, and You are somehow there. So I will fall in the shadow of death, and it will not harm me. For You will give your angels charge over me, to keep me in all your ways.

Now as I approach the center of the earth, I know You are with me. The great waters close over my head, and I die. Then as I come into my own death, I find a tiny door marked "Open me."

After her free fall and the long moment in the abyss, Lady Zane came to rest beside a narrow door. She knelt down and looked through it into the loveliest garden she had ever seen. She longed to get through the narrow door but did not know how to do so.

First she thought that getting through the little door might be a matter of size, but then she realized she didn't know how to arrange a change of size. She was large. The door was small. Her arms and legs would not even begin to fit through it.

"Even if I could get my head through the doorway, it would be of very little use without my shoulders," she thought.

She looked about for a solution, some potion she could drink, some instrument to pry her way in. After awhile, some lines from Emily Dickinson came to mind: "Prayer is the little implement /

Through which men reach / Where presence is denied them."

All at once it became clear to her that she was meant for the garden, that her desire for the garden was her assurance of getting in.

"I only have to believe," she said aloud to no one in particular. "And then I will be there."

CHAPTER SEVEN

Passing Over, Passing Through

In which Lady Zane learns
to live in two kingdoms
at the same time.

Z ane came then into the inward kingdom. Without being told, she knew it
was possible to live there and in the outward kingdom at the same time.

In the outward kingdom there were tasks to be
done. It was necessary to cook breakfast, make lists,
go to the grocery store, step into automobiles and
drive to work, attend meetings, outline agendas,
write and read reports, carry briefcases, prepare
briefs to go into the briefcases (or whatever docu-
ments might fill up the cases to a respectable level
of fatness), have oil changed in the car, and have
the gas tank filled from time to time.

Also, in the outward kingdom it was necessary
to have confrontations, seek advantage, take
chances and risks, finance ventures and make

deals, invest and protect investments, strive and grasp, manage and utilize, and, most important, to win.

Mind you, there was a person in her, a part of her, that loved the outward kingdom. All that furious activity and achievement! Building, planning, arranging, managing, pressing on, pushing forward, setting up goals and strategies. But she also loved the peace of the inward kingdom. There it was possible not merely to live but also to dwell, to exist, to wait, to let go, to rest, to be still, and to surrender—to possess nothing and everything, to care and not to care.

"Isn't it better in that inward kingdom, where I can dwell with the Lord all the days of my life?" she wanted to know.

"But what if it were possible," Lady Zane thought, "to be two people? One who lives in the outward kingdom and another who lives in the inward kingdom—to be both persons at one time?"

"I advise you to leave off this minute!" She generally gave herself very good advice (though she seldom followed it) and sometimes she scolded herself so severely as to bring tears into her eyes; and once she remembered trying to box her own ears for having cheated herself at a game of croquet she was playing against herself, for this curious child was very fond of trying to be two people. "But it's no use now," thought poor Alice, "to pretend to be two people! Why, there's hardly enough of me left to make *one* respectable person!"

Wasn't she like Alice in Wonderland? Wasn't she struggling, as Alice had, with the wish to be two people at the same time? Had Lewis Carroll grasped her true identity, born to the purple, born to wear a crown?

What wert thou, dream-Alice, in thy foster-father's eyes? How shall he picture thee? Loving, first, loving and gentle: loving as a dog (forgive the prosaic simile, but I know no earthly love so pure and perfect) and gentle as a fawn: then courteous—courteous to *all*, high or low, grand or grotesque, King or Caterpillar, even as though she were herself a King's daughter, and her clothing of wrought gold: then trustful, ready to accept the wildest impossibilities with all that utter trust that only dreamers know; and lastly, curious—wildly curious, and with the eager enjoyment of life that comes only in the happy hours of childhood, when all is new and fair, and when Sin and Sorrow are but names—empty names signifying nothing!

So she went on, day after day, living in the inward kingdom and the outward kingdom at the same time, without mentioning her guilty secret to a living soul.

"It's no use pretending. Everyone sees right through you," said the Inner Voice, which was often fond of interrupting her just when she began to feel pompous about herself.

"Do they? I thought I had them completely fooled," Lady Zane replied, explaining how carefully she had separated the two halves of her life, the outward and the inward parts.

"Outwardly, you're pretending to be a totally worldly person. But I know better," said the Inner Voice.

"But I am worldly. I'm completely worldly. I love pretty dresses, and tape decks, and going to parties, and having a good time. Those things are worldly. And I like them. Doesn't that make me worldly?" Lady Zane inquired.

"Not entirely," the Inner Voice responded. "You are worldly in a legitimate sense, when you own things—provided you don't allow them to own you."

"I used to be driven by worldly things—success, power, sex. I wanted them, more than anything. I thought I would triumph if only I could gain those things."

"And now, I suppose, you are above temptation?"

"Not at all. But there's something much more difficult about the temptations I have now," Zane said.

"And what is that?"

"They are extremely subtle. Now that I have passed over into the inward kingdom, where holiness is possible, sex and liquor and power trips aren't nearly as attractive. But I'm afraid that something else, something far more terrifying, may slip me up along the way."

"It's a wise child who knows her own tempter," the Inner Voice responded.

There was a sudden silence. Zane waited for the Inner Voice to speak again, but there was nothing.

"Cloudy will miss me very much tonight, I should think." (Cloudy was her cat, whose full name was the Cloudy of Unknowing.) I hope they'll remember her saucer of Tender Vittles when it's time," she thought. "Cloudy, I hope you miss me as much as I miss you, my dear," she said, drowsily, for in the inward kingdom it was sometimes difficult to remain alert.

"Praying is so exhausting," Lady Zane sighed. "I forget who I am. I forget who the Lord is. I forget what He is saying to me. I forget which technique of prayer I am supposed to be using. I forget my breathing exercises. I forget my mantra, my spiritual journal, my Myers-Briggs, my Kiersey Sorter, my copy of *The Spiritual Exercises*, my *Bible Verses for Today*."

After a while, she tried to remember a verse of Scripture, just to be sure that she was not merely drifting lazily through the kingdom of prayer.

She felt, being of Anglo-American heritage, that an industrious attitude was always appropriate.

My mind to me a kingdom is,
Such present joys therein I find,
That it excels all other bliss
That earth affords, or grows by kind:

Some have too much and still do crave;
I little have, and seek no more;
They poor, I rich; they beg, I give;
They lack, I have; they pine, I live.

How odd, she thought. For the words that came to mind were not Scripture at all. But nevertheless they were all about riches and poverty, just as the Scripture was. "Do you suppose the Lord is speaking to me through literature as well?" she wanted to know.

But the Inner Voice would not answer. Perhaps it was not going to let her be two persons. She would have to live as one person in both kingdoms.

So that was what was meant by passing over. And all this while she had assumed that it was what the Israelites did when they left the kingdom of Egypt and entered the Promised Land.

"You have it entirely wrong, dearest heart," chirped the Inner Voice, fussy at having been provoked again. "When the Israelites left Egypt, they went into the wilderness for forty years. It was a long time before they entered the Promised Land."

"Oh, you are so particular about historical details," Lady Zane said crankily. "When everyone knows the historicity of the Bible is highly controversial."

"Ah, perhaps," the Inner Voice retorted. "But the truth of the Bible is not."

Lady Zane's Outer Voice was quiet for a few moments. She had no interest in getting into a scriptural debate, and besides, she felt sure it was a definite distraction from prayer.

Again, she reached into her memory for words that would lead her back into the inward kingdom, away from rational discourse and into the experience of prayer.

And Mary said, My soul doth magnify the Lord,
And my spirit hath rejoiced in God my Saviour.
For he that is mighty hath done to me great things;
and holy is his name.

A great wave of peacefulness suddenly broke over her and she knew herself to be speaking with the Lord.

"You have put down the mighty from their thrones," she said.

"And exalted those of low degree," said the Lord.

"The hungry you have filled with good things," she said.

"And the rich I have sent empty away," replied the Lord.

"You have come to the help of Israel your servant," she said.

"According to the promise I made to your ancestors, of my mercy to Abraham and to his descendants for ever," the Lord finished.

Then there was silence in the inward kingdom for the space of about half an hour.

After a long time, Lady Zane left off praying and reached for her spiritual notebook, where she wrote the following words:

> What, then, are we ordinary folk
> to do with ourselves?
> How can we be instruments of
> compassion and change?
>
> When we pray, we can pray
> not only for ourselves,
> not only for justice and peace,
> not only for our cherished agendas,
> but for openness to a deeper
> understanding, a new compassion—
> conversion.

We can pray to become children of the promise.

To inherit the kingdom promised to us
from the foundation of the world.

And this kingdom is an inward kingdom.
But it is not to be found by walling up or running
away.
Instead, this kingdom turns us outward to others.
And makes it possible for us to see meaning
in the events and issues of our times.

We are travelers then.
Passing over and passing through.
Into a kingdom of heightened consciousness
and concern for others.
A greater poverty of spirit,
a deeper purity of heart.
Not a kingdom of thinking
or of dreaming and knowing,
at least not entirely,

but a kingdom of chasing
and following and responding,
of transforming and being transformed.
A kingdom where if a beggar asks for your shirt,
you give him your cloak also.
And you feel the richer for having done so.
A kingdom so bound together in love
that even peace and global understanding seem
possible.

The pencil had worn down to a nubbin, and the
hard work of writing with an old-fashioned pencil
was making a sore place on her index finger. Lady

Zane stopped, read over what she had written once or twice, and closed the book, wondering whether anyone else in the universe could possibly understand.

She thought it was unlikely. But all the same she was certain she must continue her journey.

CHAPTER EIGHT

Mousedom

In which Lady Zane is invited
to a royal ball, and
the justice of God to the lowly
is made clear.

"Mine is a long and sad tale!" said the
Mouse, turning to Alice, and sighing.

"It is a long tail, certainly," said Alice, looking
down with wonder at the Mouse's tail; "but why do
you call it sad?" And she kept on puzzling about it
while the Mouse was speaking, so that her idea of the
tale was something like this:

"Fury said to
a mouse, That
he met
in the
house,
'Let us
both go
to law:
I will
prosecute
you—
Come, I'll
take no
denial;
We must
have a
trial:
For
really
this
morning
I've
nothing
to do.
Said the
mouse to
the cur,
'Such a
trial,
dear sir,
With no
jury or
judge,
would be
wasting
our breath.'
'I'll be
judge.
I'll be
jury,'
Said
cunning
old Fury:
'I'll try
the whole
cause
and
condemn
you
to
death.'"

Now Lady Zane and Companions found themselves confronted with a new quandary in the form of an invitation. It was quite remarkable: large and square, perhaps twelve by twelve inches, and the envelope was sealed with an elaborate seal embedded in bright red wax. Within the envelope was an announcement that read:

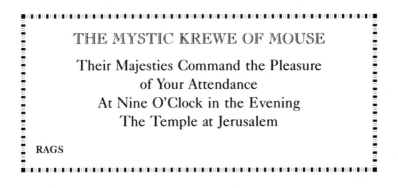

THE MYSTIC KREWE OF MOUSE

Their Majesties Command the Pleasure
of Your Attendance
At Nine O'Clock in the Evening
The Temple at Jerusalem

RAGS

"How odd," said Lady Zane, for there was a quirkiness about the invitation. Certainly she was invited to a ball, but when? And while she had seen, out of the corner of her eye, a rather plain building with mysterious neon design known about the city as the Jerusalem Temple, it seemed to her far more likely that the temple in question was the Temple at Jerusalem, which had been destroyed some years after the birth of the Lord and which would not, if prophecies were correct, be restored until the end of the world.

"But what if it were the end?" said the Cougar, feeling rather vulnerable whenever he heard talk about the end of the world.

"Nonsense. If it were the end, they would certainly not put out engraved invitations," said Zane.

"What is even more suspicious is the note here in the lefthand corner about attire," Cougar insisted.

"Rags? How silly," said Lady Zane, for she had overlooked it on first reading, thinking it said RSVP.

"What sort of a ball would one be invited to in rags?" she wondered out loud.

"A royal ball. In Mousedom," replied the Coachman, drawing his carriage up to the curb.

Lady Zane and her companions felt an odd sensation. For the Coachman was definitely a mouse, yet he was much larger than they.

"Have you come to take us there?" they asked.

"All in good time," he said. "For the hour cometh, and now is, when the children of the Kingdom shall dance before the Lord in wisdom and in truth."

"I don't understand," said Lady Zane. "If it is a social occasion, there certainly are rules, aren't there?"

"Of course," replied the Coachman. "But as with all exclusive societies, the rules are unwritten. The eligible members and their guests simply know what to do."

"Then we have been invited into an exclusive society?" she asked.

"Exclusive and secret. A kingdom of justice and peace. And only the little children will get in."

Lady Zane looked down and saw that she was wearing the most exquisite rags anyone had ever seen. They were tattered and worn, and the dress seemed to have been worn in the sunshine and the cotton fields until it was faded beyond belief.

She saw, too, that her hands were dark and the palms only were pink. And her companions had also changed so that she barely recognized them.

She could hear the fiddles tuning up, and there were sounds of humming in the distance.

"Hurry, there's so little time," the Coachman said, "the Grand March will definitely be beginning."

The coach sped through the darkness, and Lady Zane hardly knew where they were going. Rain splattered the panes of the coach windows, and the raindrops glittered like diamonds. The drops drummed on the roof, making an ominous sound. Her heart beat thunderously, and she wished the jouncing ride—over cobblestones and uneven bricks, she supposed—would soon be over.

"Miss Dorothy Alice Melanie Zane Mouse," said the Master of Ceremonies, as Lady Zane was swept into the great ballroom for the march.

"She was a Hamilton on her mother's side," Lady Zane heard someone saying, as the tiers upon tiers of the Mouse Temple twittered with applause.

The room was crowded with mice of every degree of honor. There were Duke Mice, their gold plumes nodding; there were Page Mice, following behind and adjusting the royal trains. There were Masker Mice, the ordinary members of the Krewe, scampering about the floor in frisky attitudes; there were Majesty Mice, the King and Queen themselves, presiding over the scene with elegant aplomb.

"Does it mean anything to be presented at court," Lady Zane wanted to know, as a courtly Duke Mouse approached her, offering his arm.

"Not every court is important. But this is the most exclusive in the history of the world, ma'am," he said with confidence.

"And what must one do to be invited?" inquired Lady Zane.

"The only way in is by the path of humility," he answered. "By your presence here, you acknowledge that you are willing to be crucified."

Then Lady Zane understood that she had come into Mousedom not by any doing of her own but by a special grace. And she clapped her hands with delight.

Then the Mouse Musicians struck up a tune, and it made her feel like dancing.

> In a house, in a street, in a quadrant,
> In a street, in a lane, in a road.

You turn to the left on the right hand,
And there is my true love's abode.
I go there a-courting
And croon to my love like a dove
And swearing on my bended knee
If ever I cease to love
May the moon be turned into green cheese
If ever I cease to love.

Now, from every side of the ballroom, the musicians began to march. They carried with them their trumpets and tubas and oompa-paahed their way through the room.

She can sing
She can play the piano
She can jump, she can dance, she can run.
She is a wonderful girlee.
She's all of them rolled into one.
I adore her beauty
Like an angel dropped from above.
May fish get legs and cows lay eggs
If ever I cease to love.
May all dogs wag their tails in front
May we all turn into cats and dogs
If ever I cease to love.

Then the King of the Mystic Krewe of Mouse descended from his glittering throne and approached Lady Zane with a look of mischief and delight.

He swept her around the floor in a waltz so swift it left her panting, then concluded his dance with a royal bow. As the dance ended, the Mouse King pressed a small velvet box into her hand. She opened it, and found there a ring, just her size.

"Wear it as a sign of your priesthood and kingship," the Mouse King twittered. "For the time of the Lord is near at hand."

The words—*noblesse oblige*—on the crest of the ring were engraved on her heart, for she had lived them already.

It was almost midnight, and the clock began to strike with mathematical regularity.

Lady Zane began to look around for her coach, remembering another story and wondering if her coach might have turned into a pumpkin somehow.

"This story has its own ending, Lady Zane," the Mouse King said. "There is no need to run away, for the rightful King has already found you and you are promised a place in his Kingdom."

But Zane was still not reassured. She felt a deep terror as the clock continued to strike. And she looked neither right nor left but made a wild dash down the high steps of the temple until she came into the rainwashed street, missing her fellow pilgrims but hoping they would soon find her.

CHAPTER NINE

The Arrows of Experience

━━━━━◄◆►━━━━━

In which it becomes clear
that arrows point all one way.

It was clear by now to Lady Zane that
there would be no turning back, and the
path was highly irregular.

It was impossible to describe the experience except by way of metaphor, and her need to communicate was becoming more and more insistent.

It was just at this moment that she came with her other friends into a dark wood where there were arrows pointing the way.

"Which way?" asked the Cowpoke.

"There's only one way," Lady Zane answered. "Follow the Arrow of Time."

"The what?" he continued,

"It's Eddington's arrow, pointing from yesterday to tomorrow. It was invented to explain that later is different from earlier," Zane answered.

"That's simple enough," Cowpoke thought.

"You would think so. But it gets harder," Zane

went on. "The interesting thing about time is that it can point only one way. Unlike space, which spills over in all directions."

"And which way does it point?" asked Cougar.

"From the past to the future," she said,

The others were baffled.

"You mean to say a concept was required to express this?" Nasja-the-Good wanted to know.

"And not only that," Lady Zane went on, "the arrow is irreversible."

"I understand," the Piute said.

"The only problem is, Eddington's irreversible arrow only deals with physical time. He thinks that the one-wayness of physical time, from more organization to less, ensures that the world makes sense."

"It must be all that time on the prairie," said the Cowpoke, wagging his head from side to side as if to clear his thinking. "It sounds confusing to me."

"Why confusing?"

The Piute, who knew about Eddington without having to ask, said quietly, "Eddington says that the one-way arrow points to a more chaotic future. But history shows that as time passes, more things are getting organized and sorted out. As the universe slides through centuries and millennia, new civilizations, new structures, new world orders come into being. The creative dance into novelty!"

"Very observant, Nasja-the-Good," said Lady Zane. "There are really three paradoxes. So Layzer has proposed three Arrows of Time."

The Piute was not awed. He already knew that Layzer was a Harvard astronomer.

But Cowpoke was impressed. "Doggone," he observed, somewhat under his breath.

"First is the arrow of cosmic expansion," said Nasja-the-Good, "in which the universe, all balled up in its embryonic beginning, explodes into novelty and keeps on expanding. The second is the arrow of history, in which all the galaxies, stars, and planets and life, civilization, and mind keep evolving into richer and more complex structures. And the third is the thermodynamic arrow, which points in the direction of increasing entropy."

"And what is entropy?" said Lady Zane, leading him on with delight.

"Entropy is a word invented by Claude Shannon."

"And who is Claude Shannon?"

"He is a philosopher of information," the Piute answered.

"And what is entropy?"

"It is what Shannon says it is, if it is anything at all." He was getting weary of the cat-and-mouse exchange.

"I'm not so sure about Shannon, but there is one lovely thing about Layzer," Lady Zane went on.

"He believes that the present moment always contains an element of genuine novelty and so the future is never entirely predictable."

"That sounds okay by me," said the Cowpoke.

There was a long pause, and Lady Zane and the others continued moving along the path set by the Arrows of Time.

"They didn't mention spiritual time, of course," Lady Zane added after a few moments. But then you can't expect scientists to know everything."

There was another pause.

"Funny thing about philosophers and mathematicians and other theoretical types," the Piute said after some reflection. "They tell you what you already knew."

Lady Zane smiled. She noticed that the Mountain Lion had curled up for an irreversible nap and the Cowpoke's cigarette smoke was uncurling in the same direction that time was unfurling.

"Not only that," Lady Zane said, "I am sure Layzer is right when he says that the intuitive perception of the world as unfolding in time captures one of the most deep-seated properties of the universe."

"That's deep all right," said the Cougar, flicking one ear sleepily as he spoke. He had not reversed his nap but it was clearly time for him to wake up, and the arrow was continuing to point toward the next moment.

The Entrance to Elfland

In which Lady Zane
confronts the High Corporations,
and risks losing her value
as a consultant.

When the businessman rebukes the idealism of his office boy, it is commonly in some speech such as this: "Ah, yes, when one is young, one has these ideals in the abstract and these castles in the air; but in middle age they all break up like clouds, and one comes down to a belief in practical politics, to using the machinery one has and getting on with the world as it is." But since I have grown up, I have discovered that these philanthropic old men were telling lies. They said that I should lose my ideals and begin to believe in the methods of practical politicians. Now, I have not lost my ideals in the least; what I have lost is my old childlike faith in practical politics.

The train was jammed with people, and their faces were desolate, Lady Zane thought. The impression she had was that they were on a subway hurtling into the unknown, but no one seemed the least disturbed. How she had come there was of no consequence to anyone else but herself, and on second thought, she decided it was a fine spot for meditation.

When she took a second look, she noticed that only a few faces were desolate. Others were preoccupied with newspapers, while still others were reading scriptural books in every language.

There were small books written in Hebrew, being read from right to left by men in long overcoats with curlicue sideburns and long pointy beards. There were women in kerchiefs, fingering prayer beads. There were oriental persons reading books that Lady Zane could not understand. All the people seemed alienated, but perhaps it was because they were lost in their own thoughts. They were required, by force of circumstance, to stand close to each other like cattle herded into a boxcar.

As a defense, she reached into the pocket of her gingham dress and found a little book of Scripture there.

While it was her custom to pray from the Scriptures daily, on this particular day she had no reading planned, so she opened the book at random. Her eye fell on a passage from First Corinthians.

Let those who have wives live as though they had none, and those who mourn as though they were not mourning, and those who rejoice as though they were not rejoicing, and those who buy as though they had no goods, and those who deal with the world as though they had no dealings with it.

How appropriate, she thought, as she hurtled into Manhattan with her eyes fixed on the world to come.

"Please help muscular dystrophy," screeched a woman as she came through the speeding car, her muscular dystrophy collection can extended. Her affliction was familiar to the passengers, and, by and large, they ignored it. But the sound of coins thunking into the can had a comforting sound. Lady Zane knew someone was attentive to the woman's concerns.

"Queens Plaza, change to the RR and the N trains for Manhattan," said the voice over the loudspeaker. The door against which Lady Zane was leaning opened abruptly, and she thought for a moment she would lose her balance and slip out. Between the train and the platform there were several inches, hardly enough to fall into, but nevertheless it gave her an uneasy feeling.

As they passed underneath the river, Lady Zane was afraid that the top of the tunnel would cave in and they would be flooded underground, but she knew it was a mere childhood anxiety and prayed her way through it.

This was the long part of the ride, and it seemed to go on forever. The only way to make it go faster was to stand at the front, look out the door, and watch the parallel tracks converge at infinity.

At Fifty-Third and Third, the doors opened and crowds bolted from the trains and onto the moving staircases that seemed to stretch endlessly upward.

Once she left the moving stairs, there were more stairs to climb. She noticed these were sprinkled with stardust, though nobody else seemed to be paying the slightest attention.

When she emerged from the train station, she saw beggars everywhere. Some were sleeping in the doorways. Others were sitting cross-legged on the sidewalk, rattling their cups. One of them had a Santa Claus beard, unclean and matted, and was wearing a monkish garment that seemed to come from another century.

At the doorway to the Tower of Commerce, Lady Zane presented her pass.

"The meeting of the Ad Hoc Committee of the High Corporations will be starting in just a few moments, Miss . . . ah? Your name?" said the Guard.

"It's . . . ah . . . Zane."

"Your last name, Miss . . . ah . . ."

The Guard was suspicious. He was looking at a

list of approved names for attendance at the committee meeting, and the figure of the slight girl in the gingham frock, holding her dog in a basket, was implausible to say the least. But who was he to criticize the ways of High Corporations?

"You must identify yourself, Miss, or you won't be permitted to attend the committee meeting. Security clearance procedures, strictly routine; no offense, you understand."

"I'm Zane Storey and this is my dog, Rover."

"Yes, of course, you're right here on the list," the Guard responded, issuing her a plastic ID card that could be affixed to her clothes. Zane could tell that he was rather surprised to find her name on the list.

"But it doesn't say anything about Rover," he grumbled.

"I am sure we look rather offbeat," Zane said with complete composure, "but in fact I am a freelance corporate strategy adviser." She offered these words over her shoulder as Rover growled his response. "The rest of my staff, a Cowperson and a Native American, are waiting for us at a rendezvous point," she went on, but by now the Guard had stopped protesting.

There were several banks of elevators, all going to different floors. He escorted Lady Zane and Rover to the one going to the highest floor.

"Just push the button for floor 144," he said.

Her ears began to ring as the elevator ascended higher and higher, and Rover started to whine.

But when the elevator door opened, they forgot their discomfort, for their breath was almost taken away by the luxury of their surroundings.

There were windows all around the room that on a clear day would have provided a remarkable view, perhaps as far as the upper Hudson River or even beyond. But as luck would have it, the fog had closed in, providing an odd sense of alienation and disquietude.

Even so, the interior space was exquisite in itself. Set into each of the walls were tiny three-dimensional rooms depicting scenes in the history of commerce. In the center of the room were statues of great leaders of commerce—Rockefeller, Carnegie, Mellon, Morgan.

Lady Zane looked around for Michael, but he was nowhere in sight. So she simply followed her nose down the long corridor toward the Committee Room.

The members of the Ad Hoc Committee were assembling, and each one's place at the table was clearly indicated.

Lady Zane couldn't help noticing how much her washed-out cotton dress clashed with the pinstriped suits of the other members, but no one seemed to mind. She soon found a place with her name on a card: "Zane Storey, Creative Strategist, Member at Large."

The place was inviting; she found an agenda, a lined pad of paper, sharpened pencils, a glass of water, and pamphlets and leaflets. Curious, she snuggled into a chair.

The publicly owned corporation for profit had its origins in Great Britain.

Lady Zane read from a small pamphlet beside her place. It was called "Views on Corporate Responsibility" by Edward Harness.

In all countries where such corporations exist, the right to that existence rests on legislation created by government to achieve a very few simple aims for the common good. Prior to the passage of such enabling legislation, one person could join with another in a business venture only through the route of unlimited partnership. In such partnerships, the risk of failure was too great in many instances. Each partner was liable for all of his or her personal assets in the event of collapse. . . .

In addition, the creation of this paper citizen, the corporation, allowed an entity to exist which could be relatively free from the mortality of man. As the investors died off, the paper entity could live on and continue to perform its intended function. . . .

The corporation was required in order to get bigger jobs done—jobs which society needed done—than individuals alone could do. Said another way, the state created the corporation to enhance society's well-being. . . .

The corporation—as I have said earlier—is a paper citizen, and every citizen has a responsibility to his fellow citizen. Democratic society is based on that fact. The corporation cannot ignore that truth any more than an individual being can. . . .

The state provides a corporation with the opportunity to earn a profit if it meets society's needs. It follows inevitably that reported profits are the primary scorecard that tells the world how well a corporation is meeting its basic responsibility to society.

I said earlier that we had a record of fulfilling our responsibility to the communities where we operate. I believe this is true, but I will have to admit that there are times when it is hard to define and quantify our responsibility. How much of our shareholders' money should the managers of the business give away in the interest of higher education, and to the United Way campaigns of our base communities? To the fostering of culture and the arts? How much should we spend in money and time attempting to persuade the public to adequately finance public schools, or to help reorganize local government?

The Chairperson called the meeting to order.

"We're here to consider the matter of the Pied Piper, which has been plaguing us for some time," the Chairperson said.

"Permit me to review the issues briefly so that the members may offer a viewpoint on the proper course of action.

"It seems that some time ago this raggle-taggle fellow approached us with a proposal to eliminate the rats that were infesting the sewers of our city.

"You may recall this was a severe problem, and our committee was put together because there was a suggestion that some of the industrial practices of our respective organizations may have been making the situation worse.

"Now the rat infestation problem the Piper alleged to remove has in fact cleared up. And our understanding is that, as far as we know, he had nothing to do with it.

"But he insists that since we contracted with him for it, even though the problem has been solved, the resolution is because of his intervention and we are therefore responsible to him for an exorbitant sum, which is far in excess of what we presume the members of this committee—which is of course merely an informal group, with no legal identity or consequent liability—er, ah, of what we presume the members of this committee would deem appropriate for their respective organizations to pay."

"And what is the price he is asking?" one member asked.

"You really want to know?" The Chairperson responded.

"Yes, by all means," said the member.

"He is asking us to eliminate poverty and homelessness," was the Chairperson's answer.

Immediately there was laughter. And then a murmur of disbelief ran around the room, followed by giggling, muffled coughs, even sneezes. Every conceivable physical expression of surprise suitable to a high committee member was heard.

"By the terms of our agreement with him, does he have the right to ask this?"

"In fact, he says he has a moral obligation. You see, I'm afraid . . . that in our panic over the escalation of the rats and our despair about the possibility of the Piper's actually solving the problem, we permitted him to name his own price."

"And he has done so?"

"Precisely."

"Pardon me, pardon me," Zane said, trying hard to get the Chairperson's attention, "I was wondering if . . . well, what I mean is, why don't we simply do it? It seems to me like a very good idea."

"Good idea? Why, it's an outrageous idea."

"It's never been done before. It's totally out of the question."

"Eliminate poverty? That's totally impractical. Why, you might as well set out to eliminate war!"

"One thing at a time," said Zane, with a confidence that indicated she thought the High Corporations were equal to both tasks. "I mean, wouldn't we really like to see poverty eliminated? Isn't it awkward to see those people with matted hair, living out of garbage cans and sleeping on park benches?"

"Of course we would. But after all, Madam Committeeperson, we are privately held organizations. The elimination of poverty is a matter of the common good, the public welfare. The boundaries of corporate responsibilities may not stretch far enough to give us this authority."

"Mr. Chairperson, I know I am naive. But my naiveté is carefully chosen, assumed when desperation was becoming the prevailing style. I propose to be a style leader, a creative advancer into novelty. My powers of invention are all I have to bring to this committee. And if I am not mistaken, that is why you have invited me here."

A silence fell. Everyone in the room was suddenly all ears.

"You see, Mr. Chairperson, I don't raise this issue as a reprimand. I am not willing to blame the High Corporations for all the ills that flesh is heir to. Instead, I believe in all of you—in your power to design, to innovate, to strategize. It is not only a matter of high technology. It is also a matter of high courage and high imagination. Mind you, I don't want the government to shirk its responsibility, but I believe in you.

"I know the obstacles are great. There is sludge. There is absurdity. There is graft. There is lying. There is distortion. There is deception. There is wickedness. There is corruption. Maybe worst of all, there is bias, which makes what ought to get better get worse instead. But still, I think that of all the organizations on earth, the High Corporations are the ones that keep believing."

Almost in spite of himself, and in violation of proper meeting procedure, the Chairperson began to respond: "Well, I believe in some things. In the art of the possible. In the possibility of profitability. In the separation of church and state. In the appropriateness of the private sector not getting mixed up with the public sector."

"I think you have stopped believing that all things are possible with God," said Zane.

"Ms. Storey, I do understand that you are a legitimate member of this group and that you are considered a fine strategist, but frankly I am in some doubt as to how this naive line of reasoning will bring us to any practical conclusions."

"Pardon me, Mr. Chairperson, but I have a statement I would like to read into the record."

"By all means."

Then Zane stood up and read as follows: "A Reading from the Book of Deuteronomy."

Take heed lest you forget the Lord your God, by not keeping his commandments and his ordinances and his statutes, which I command you this day:

Lest, when you have eaten and are full, and have built goodly houses and live in them;

And when your herds and flocks multiply, and your silver and gold is multiplied;

Then your heart be lifted up, and you forget the Lord your God, who brought you out of the land of Egypt, out of the house of bondage;

Who led you through the great and terrible wilderness, with its fiery serpents and scorpions and thirsty ground where there was no water; who brought you water out of the flinty rock;

Who fed you in the wilderness with manna which your fathers did not know, that he might humble you and test you, to do your good in the end.

Beware lest you say in your heart, "My power and the might of my hand have gotten me this wealth."

You shall remember the Lord your God, for it is he who gives you power to get wealth, that he may confirm his covenant which he swore to your fathers, as at this day.

And if you forget the Lord your God and go after other Gods, and serve them and worship them, I solemnly warn you this day that you will surely perish.

Like the nations that the Lord makes to perish before you, so shall you perish, because you would not obey the voice of the Lord your God.

"You are quite out of order, Ms. Storey," the Chairperson said. He had been trying to interrupt her for some time without success.

"But I believe I am quite in order," she replied staunchly.

Around them in the room a chorus of sounds arose, signalling a widespread discontent. Watches and beepers, being worn by the various members, began to chirp and buzz. Pressures from outside were building to an intolerable high. Calls could no longer be held; stock market investments were clamoring to be dealt with; the world outside the room seemed to be in chaos. Lady Zane's time was assuredly up.

"Let the record show," Zane persisted, "that at one moment in history there was one person who believed in your dream even when you had forgotten to believe it."

"You will not be invited back, Zane," said one of the other members, mournfully. "You have been a valued member until now, but the level of your dissent is becoming unacceptable."

Lady Zane's heart was beating crazily. She scooped Rover back into his basket with a show of courage, but she feared they might be mobbed by the rest of the group.

As she went down in the elevator she felt a new sense of freedom. She knew she had been impractical. She was sad at the loss of dear friends and colleagues with whom she could never collaborate again. How she wished she could convince them that she believed in them. Instead, they would feel betrayed, as though she had spurned them.

But at least she had expressed what was in her heart. Now they were free to choose. In good conscience she and the others could go on to the next part of the journey.

CHAPTER ELEVEN

What Wonderful Windmills

In which the Pilgrims are
confronted with Earthly Perfection
and find themselves mystified.

When the travelers came into the country of the windmills, they were struck with a vision of superb beauty. Before them, in a scene of pastoral perfection, the hills and valleys rolled, and tiny towns were set in the country side. Over them were the towering presences of great and harmonious machines, standing guard, as it seemed, over the populace, and toiling with great simplicity and courage on behalf of society's goals.

"What wonderful windmills," Lady Zane observed.

But a second thought occurred to her. Weren't these the creatures against which Don Quixote had done battle? But now they looked so peaceful and befriending, so protective and strong.

Then she remembered the encounter between the Count de Guiche and Cyrano de Bergerac.

"Windmills, if you fight with them," de Guiche had said, "will throw you down into the mire."

Cyrano had responded: "Or up, into the stars."

It was clear to her that she wanted to follow Cyrano up into the stars. But how? By what method was progress to be made?

Could one climb, somehow, on the arms of the windmills? Admittedly, they were breathtaking. Giants with moving arms, their energy fitful yet peaceful, they seemed to be just waiting for a puff of wind.

"Who lives here, in the country of the windmills?" Lady Zane wanted to know.

"People who believe in alternative sources of power," said the others.

"Then perhaps we are in California," said Lady Zane.

And there, in black and white on the side of one of the windmills, was a sign that read:

Press Conference

CALIFORNIA JUSTICE

Come meet and talk with
leaders of the wind industry.

Underneath the sign was what seemed to be a newspaper clipping, though it was worn and tattered and blotched in places, which made for difficult reading.

WINDVALE, CALIFORNIA. Key wind industry leaders met here today to announce the globalization of wind technology in a fast-growing effort that is soon to reach into every corner of the civilized world.

To make their point, the industry leaders cited the State of California.

"Small, innovative firms here have installed almost 8,500 turbines throughout the state, producing enough energy for 70,000 modern homes," an industry spokesman said.

"By the end of this year, we predict developers will have built over 1,000 megawatts of wind capacity, the equivalent of a large nuclear reactor. The commission also expects wind machines to supply at least 8 percent of the state's electric power by century's end, enough electricity to run all the homes in Los Angeles.

"Well-designed machines placed at windy sites generate electric power for less than ten cents per kilowatt hour, making it cheaper than power from coal or nuclear plants," another industry spokesman stated. "In fact," said one source, who declined to be identified, "developers cut costs per kilowatt in half between 1981 and 1984, and they continue experimenting with a variety of designs, including vertical axis machines that look like inverted eggbeaters."

There might have been more to the newspaper article, but the fragment posted on the side of the windmill ended there. There was an uncomfortable silence. The little band of friends looked around. There was no one in sight but the windmills themselves, and it was easy to see how Don Quixote had confused them with giants. They stood, massive and imposing, row upon row across the picturesque terrain, their arms moving with the grace and precision of wind warriors. But there were no humans in sight.

The friends continued walking. After a while they came across an old woman in wooden shoes. She was sweeping the front of her walk with great attention and concern.

"What time is the press conference, ma'am?" they asked.

The woman stopped and leaned on her broom, seemingly grateful for the interruption. Lady Zane saw it was an old-fashioned broom, made of twigs and stalks bound together on a long wood handle. Her face was round and cheerful, and she had bright red cheeks and lively eyes.

"Let me see now. When do they have them? Oh, they have them every once in a while. But not so often that you'd notice. You see, we haven't needed them so much since the Wind Coalition took over."

"The Wind Coalition? What is that?" Zane asked.

"They're free-spirited citizens who believe in wind. They've solved all our problems since they came to power," the old woman went on.

"All your problems? Do you like that?"

"Well, seems like in the old days folks was always fussing and fighting about something. Looked like they just loved to get into a squabble. If it wasn't coal, it was nuclear power. Then it was the water supply. And earthquakes. The number of arguments I've heard about earthquakes."

"Nobody argues about wind?" Cowpoke asked.

"Seems like there isn't much to argue about. Either it blows or it doesn't. See, here in Windvale you're really at the mercy of God."

"But isn't that true most everywhere?" Slim the Cougar wanted to know.

"It is, but folks don't realize it till they get mixed up with something as unpredictable as wind."

"Just a minute," Zane objected. "According to this newspaper article, there is now a wind technology. Wind can be controlled and predicted."

Just then, a scrap of newspaper blew into the yard.

"As evidence of the industry's increasing reliability and productivity," the newspaper article read, "the number of wind machines is doubling annually although the energy generation capacity is quadrupling."

"Lord, pour out your spirit and renew the face of the earth," Lady Zane thought to herself.

But the old woman went on: "Does it say in there about a boom in wind farms?"

Zane looked down through the later paragraphs. "Oh, yes. It says here 'The real boom is in wind farms, smaller turbine clusterings that are connected to an electric grid.'"

"Well, read on," the old woman said.

Lady Zane continued to read: "'The first such commercial enterprise began generating power in New Hampshire in 1981, but California boasts the most progress, with thousands of wind energy machines lining the ridges of Altamont, San Gregorio, and Tehachapi passes. Smaller wind farms have been developed in Vermont, Hawaii, Oregon, New York, and Montana; industry analysts expect activity soon in the Rocky Mountain States and in Texas.'"

"Well, this should be a big hit in Chicago," Lady Zane said, remembering that Chicago was known as the windy city. But she had trouble imagining whether hurricanes through the Gulf states would be a resource or a nightmare.

Just then, a rather fat man on a bicycle came into view. He was wearing a blue outfit and Chinese shoes. He stopped, huffing and puffing, then folded his bike into the shape and size of a pocket handkerchief and put it in his pocket. Before doing so, he removed a bandanna-style handkerchief and began mopping his brow.

"Am I late? Have you been waiting long? These wind clocks are so unreliable," he said.

"Late for what?" the Mountain Lion said. "There wasn't any time posted."

"Yes, but I have these inner feelings that drive me. I feel such a sense of obligation to the industry, you know."

"The industry?"

"The wind brokers, they're my employers, you see. And it's my obligation to keep the public informed about wind power. But usually there's so little public to inform, since everyone here knows about wind. But you . . . why you just wandered in."

"It's true. We're not quite sure how we did that, but we've come a long way, and we always heard that the windmills were the downfall of Don Quixote."

"Balderdash! That was a story cooked up by the opposition, who were extremely hostile to the wind interests of the sixteenth century," the wind spokesman explained.

"Wind interests? In the sixteenth century?" Zane asked.

"She who does not understand wind history is condemned to repeat it," said the wind spokesman.

"Aren't you aware of the number of rude jokes that have been used over the centuries about wind? Windbags, passing wind, blowhards, and so forth?"

"Why, yes, but it never occurred to me . . . " Zane responded.

"Aha! Of course. You are politically naive. Those apparently trivial expressions are part of a long-range historical process, an effort on the part of those in charge of the status quo to undermine the credibility of the Wind Revolution. But I am happy to say all that is long ago over and done with."

"The Wind Revolution?" All Zane's companions showed surprise.

Now the wind spokesman saw his chance to explain, "You see, wind belongs to the people. It is a people's power source. It has been for centuries. Way back in Don Quixote's time, when wind was a viable energy source, there were schemes afoot to discredit wind power, to make it seem like a foolhardy, impractical enterprise."

"But Cervantes was an artist, not a politician," Zane objected.

"Don't be naive. As anyone knows, art is political."

"Well, even if it is, wasn't Cervantes an enlightened fellow trying to make fun of the bombast of chivalry?"

"All I have to say is, anyone who makes a fool out of windmills has to tangle with me. I'm here to set the record straight on a technology that has been misunderstood, overlooked, and laughed at for generations, and to explain how people can claim their birthright by learning which way the wind blows." The wind spokesman was warming up.

He began to press pamphlets and brochures about wind power into their hands.

> Wind Power Made Simple
> For the Aggressive Entrepreneur
>
> Wind Power and the Bottom Line
>
> Making a Profit from Wind

Nasja-the-Good looked around for a straight twig and started making his press release into a pinwheel. Meanwhile, the Cowpoke was folding his copy into a paper glider and tossing it into the breeze.

Lady Zane looked over her press packet, the pamphlets and the press release, thoughtfully. But somehow she was saddened to think that wind would be harnessed and used this way. Was it really better to use wind instead of coal and nuclear power? But after awhile she remembered a nursery rhyme and said it quietly to herself until she felt better.

> Blow, wind, blow! And go, mill, go!
> That the miller may grind his
> corn;
> That the baker may take it
> And into rolls make it,
> And bring us some hot in the
> morn.

The travelers continued walking peacefully over hill and dale looking for the edge of the country of the windmills. It was only then that they began to feel an odd sense of being watched, even of being held captive there. Perhaps the windmills were really sophisticated border guards who would not let them go.

"Why do you want to leave us? Everything is perfection here," Lady Zane heard a voice saying, but she couldn't identify the source of it. Was it possible that the voice was speaking in her head, some kind of thought transference?

The Cougar, who was in the lead, approached one of the windmills and was startled to find the blades of it swooping down so that he could not pass by.

"They want to keep us here by force, if necessary," the Piute said. "We are not as free as we thought after all." Fearless though he was, the circling blades intimidated him.

"Let me try it first," said the Cowpoke. "I'm tough as a tanned hide." He ambled up to one of the windmills and was suddenly seized by its blades and circled through the air down, as the Count de Guiche had said, into the mire.

"It doesn't hurt," he explained. "It's just like being thrown from a buckin' bronco. Who do these machines think they are, anyway?"

"They could be God's representatives," said Lady Zane. "After all, isn't the Holy Spirit sort of a wind that blows?"

"We never think of things like that," the Cowpoke said. "That's more your line."

But would God's secret agents be so hostile? Lady Zane wasn't sure. "The windmills either want to stop our journey here, or they want to take us somewhere," she decided.

"I guess we have to pray our way through the border of the windmill territory," she said.

So the little group prayed. At first it seemed that nothing much was happening. But soon there was a hush.

The wind was dropping. Slower and slower turned the great blades of the windmills until at last they came to rest. The giants were framed against the sky, perfectly still.

Then the friends, carrying their press packets with them, passed safely under the great blades of the windmills and into the next adventure.

CHAPTER TWELVE

Into the Side of the Mountain

In which Michael Archangel shows Lady Zane and the Pilgrims a glimpse of judgment.

Into the street the Piper stept
Smiling first a little smile
As if he knew what magic slept
Into his quiet pipe the while;
Then, like a musical adept,
To blow the pipe his lips he wrinkled,
And green and blue his sharp eyes twinkled,
Like a candle-flame where salt is sprinkled. . . .

Once more he stept into the street
And to his lips again
Laid his long pipe of smooth straight cane;
And ere he blew three notes (such sweet
Soft notes as yet musician's cunning
Never gave the enraptured air)
There was a rustling that seemed like a bustling
Of merry crowds justling at pitching and hustling,
Small feet were pattering, wooden shoes clattering,
Little hands clapping and little tongues chattering,

And, like fowls in a farmyard where barley is
scattering,
Out came the children running.
All the little boys and girls,
With rosy cheeks and flaxen curls
And sparkling eyes and teeth like pearls,
Tripping and skipping, ran merrily after
The wonderful music with shouting and laughter.

Then Michael led the travelers on, even though the crowds were flowing beside them in a great multitude. The travelers were weary and sore, but their hearts were high. They could feel the blood thumping in their veins. Clearly, something momentous was happening, and they were glad to be part of it.

In the great crowd they saw people surging from every corner of the world, dressed in garments of every country and of every color and design.

They said to the Archangel, "What is it?"

And he answered, "It is the end of time."

They looked around, not fearfully, but eagerly, and saw a great bridge, like a rainbow, stretching across the chasm, and there were multitudes walking on it.

Then Lady Zane clapped her hands and said, "It is the rainbow bridge of concepts, unifying everything."

"I think it is also something else, Zane," said Nasja-the-Good. "It looks like Nonnezochei, the rainbow bridge of my ancestors, seen only by a very few and leading to a place where one can unravel the mystery of things."

Michael rejoiced with them. For he could see in these two, and the Cowboy and the Cougar, how all things were coming together, coinciding, fusing, and uniting contradictory meanings from east and west, north and south, in one complete reconciliation.

"The time of peace is at hand. It is the end. And soon you will enter into your inheritance and be face to face with God."

But Michael was unprepared for the sorrow that swept over Lady Zane. She stood on the high cliff, holding her straw basket and wept with great heaving sobs. Beside her, Rover was yelping and yipping, too, as if his yelps and yips could offer her some comfort.

"What is the matter, Zane? You should not be sad now, for the Kingdom of God is at hand."

But Zane wept, uncontrollably. She saw them all, going across the rainbow bridge: the sick and the friendless, the halt and the lame, the blind leading the blind, and those who had been unjustly treated.

She saw the abused children, the orphans and widows, and those who had lived their whole lives in illness or solitude or pain.

She saw those who had lost fortunes by means of theft or fraud and those who had been stripped of their inheritance by double-dealing.

She saw abandoned wives and children who had been deserted and children whose lives had been taken from them before they were born.

She saw those who had died of starvation, their bodies wasting away, and some who had died of new diseases, unknown in early times. She saw the lepers, coming in groups.

She saw the criminally insane—murderers, rapists, and human butchers who had performed experiments in concentration camps.

They came by the hundreds and the thousands, streaming toward the rainbow bridge. There were so many; they were like swarms of locusts or bees, blackening the air.

Lady Zane wept as she had never wept before. Then she heard a great rushing of wings, and she looked up but could see nothing.

"What is it, Michael?"

"These are those who have survived the great period of trial. Their sins are forgiven them, and they will cross the rainbow bridge and enter in."

"But the sounds of the wings? Those unearthly sounds?"

"Those are the angels who have been appointed as special servants of the Lamb. And when the last day comes, they will be at his side, waiting to do his will."

Then Michael saw Zane's face turn ashen with fear, and she buried her face in her hands.

"Michael," she said, "I am terrified."

Michael answered, "Lady Zane, you have nothing to fear."

Ahead of her on the rainbow bridge Lady Zane saw the figure of the Piper, a merry fellow in ragged clothes of many different colors. And he was piping joyfully. Behind him was a crowd of children, skipping and laughing. Their eyes were wide with excitement.

When the band of children reached the far side of the bridge, a great door opened in the mountainside, and the children entered in.

Then, with astonishment, Lady Zane and her friends saw the mountain close as if the door had never existed. There was no trace of the children or the Piper. Everything was just as it had always been.

And when all were in to the very last
The door in the mountainside shut fast.
Did I say, all? No! One was lame
And could not dance the whole of the way;
And in after years, if you would blame
His sadness, he was used to say
"It's dull in town since my playmates left!
"I can't forget that I'm bereft
"Of all the pleasant sights they see
"Which the Piper also promised me.

"For he led us, he said, to a joyous land,
"Joining the town and just at hand,
"Where waters gushed and fruit trees grew
"And flowers put forth a fairer hue,
"And everything was strange and new;
"The sparrows were brighter than peacocks here,
"And their dogs outran our fallow deer,
"And honey bees had lost their stings,
"And horses were born with eagles' wings;
"And just as I became assured
"My lame foot would be speedily cured
"The music stopped and I stood still
"And found myself outside the hill,
"Left alone against my will,
"To go now limping as before,
"And never hear of that country more!"

"Alas for Hamelin," Michael explained. "The burghers all remembered, a bit too late, the text about the rich entering the needle's gate. Only then did they send out a call for the Piper to return. Now that they understand who he was, it will be different the next time."

"Will there be a next time, Michael?" Lady Zane was longing to know.

"You will find that out closer to the end of the journey," Michael answered.

It was hard to explain the tenderness growing between the Archangel and the Child, as though they had been meant for each other since time began.

CHAPTER THIRTEEN

Up in the Sky So Blue

In which the pilgrim children
stumble upon a place of
sublime happiness resembling
Maurice Maeterlinck's fairy tale.

How do you like to go up in a swing
Up in the air so blue?
Oh, I do think it the pleasantest thing
Ever a child can do!

Up in the air and over the wall,
Till I can see so wide,
Rivers and trees and cattle and all
Over the countryside—

Till I look down on the garden green,
Down on the roof so brown—
Up in the air I go flying again,
Up in the air and down!

All at once the pilgrim children were surrounded by bluebirds. There seemed to
be dozens, no, hundreds of them, swooping, dart-

ing, and alighting on the branches of tall pine and spruce trees.

"I think we must be near Pine Mountain, Georgia," Lady Zane said. "Because I've heard a great revival of bluebirds is going on there."

Sure enough, there was a signpost nearby. "Castaway Gardens, Home of the Georgia Bluebirds," it read.

"Come in and rest yourselves for a spell," said Jo Belle Castaway, proprietor of the Gardens.

She was fresh faced and friendly, in an offhand southern manner that Lady Zane was sure came from living way out in the country, miles from the nearest town.

"We're sure the bluebirds are coming back," said Jo Belle. "Folks like you-all are just confirming it, day after day."

"What made them disappear?" Lady Zane wanted to know.

"Our attitude," said Jo Belle. "Bluebirds are sensitive. They can tell when folks don't want them around. We cut down all the trees they were nesting in, and they plumb got disgusted. But I guess we've started to make amends."

"How long since the bluebirds started disappearing?" asked Zane.

"Oh, I reckon forty years or so—around World War II. But lately, they've just been coming back. And we are sure glad to see them."

Lady Zane, Nasja-the-Good, the Cowpoke, the Cougar, and Rover went deeper into the Georgia pines.

On one of the trees they found the following sign posted:

Happiness of the Home
Happiness of Being Well
Happiness of Pure Air
Happiness of Loving One's Parents
Happiness of the Blue Sky
Happiness of the Forest
Happiness of Sunny Hours
Happiness of Spring
Happiness of Sunsets
Happiness of Seeing
the Stars Rise
Happiness of the Rain
Happiness of the Winter Fire
Happiness of Innocent Thoughts
Happiness of Running
Barefoot in the Dew

"Dadgum it, someone sure as heck did leave a lot of happinesses here," said the Cowpoke. "Real absentminded."

Lady Zane smiled. "Maybe things are pretty spontaneous in the country of the bluebirds."

"I guess they are here for everyone to use," the Piute said. "Are they for everyone?

"My guess is, they're only for those with simplicity of heart," Lady Zane said.

"Is there some trick to it?" the others wanted to know.

"I think these happinesses have been hidden from the wise and clever and revealed to the merest children," said Zane.

"Well, that's us," said the Cougar. "We're the children."

"Then we can inherit the Kingdom prepared for us from the beginning of the world."

Then a sadness came over Lady Zane's face. "But how can we be happy when there is so much cruelty, anger, wickedness, and injustice in the world?"

And the Archangel said, "Behold, I bring you the Great Joys, which the Lord has prepared for those who love and serve him."

And they found the Great Joys etched in the stone face of a mountain.

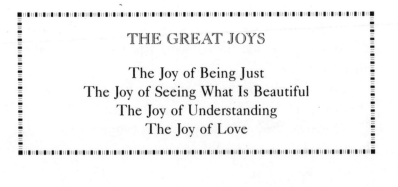

THE GREAT JOYS

The Joy of Being Just
The Joy of Seeing What Is Beautiful
The Joy of Understanding
The Joy of Love

Then a great happiness came over them, and they sensed that no one could take it away. The chorus of the bluebirds continued, praising God and saying, "Glory to God in the highest, and on earth, peace to all persons of good will."

And Lady Zane stood on top of the hill and began to recite for them:

> Happy are the poor in spirit
> Happy are they that mourn
> Happy are they who are persecuted
> for the kingdom's sake
> Happy are the peacemakers
> Happy are the meek
> Happy are the merciful
> Happy are they that hunger and
> thirst after righteousness
> Happy are you when people revile and
> persecute you and say all
> manner of evil against you
> falsely
> Rejoice and be very glad,
> for that is how they persecuted
> the prophets who were before
> you.

And when she had finished speaking, they all felt a deep sense of being one with all created things. Most especially, Zane knew that those she loved who had died were still alive in the Lord

Jesus. She could almost feel them present with her and hear their beloved voices. They were sublimely happy, and they spoke to her through the sunshine, the fresh country air, the songs of the bluebirds, and the sound of wind in the Georgia pines. And in the red earth of Georgia there was a happiness of the sunset that was like the color of heaven and bliss.

"I think my grandmother is buried here," said Lady Zane. "And my grandfather is buried with her."

And the Archangel said, "Lady Zane, your grandmother and grandfather are buried with Christ, and they have risen with him. Alleluia.

"And God shall wipe away every tear. And there will be no more sadness, neither sorrow nor pining."

CHAPTER FOURTEEN

On the Possibility That the Pied Piper Will Not Return

In which the truth of stories raises some difficulties.

The next part of the journey brought them into a large lecture hall, and Lady Zane was not at all sure how they had arrived there.

But it was pointless to reflect on it, for they were all safe and sound. Without further ado, the lecture was beginning.

There were hundreds of empty seats and only a few persons in attendance, but even so, Zane had some inkling that the lecture was momentously important, and she hurried her friends down the aisle, hoping to get a better view and a vantage point from which they could hear the lecture well.

There was a pitcher of ice water on the lectern. Three chairs were in place on the podium, but there were only two speakers to occupy them. They seemed to be distinguished persons of learning.

While waiting for the lecture to begin, Zane and her group looked around.

They were in what appeared to be a large nineteenth-century structure, with tall windows letting the sunshine in, and motes of dust drifting aimlessly through the air. The windows were bevelled in such a way that they were almost prisms. In some places the light was splitting into rainbows, and there were splotches of rose, blue, and violet painting the floor.

Inside the room there were high mirrors with elegant gilt frames and, in some places, fine oil paintings of distinguished-looking men with waistcoats and pocket watches and golden keys representing their membership in learned societies. There were marble busts of men with great heads and monumental brows, thick eyebrows knitting up in frowns of wisdom and learning. Some of the names were unknown, but Lady Zane did recognize a few of them, such as Beethoven and Bach, Descartes and Darwin, Plato and Pascal, Aristotle and Anaximander, Heraclitus and Socrates.

"Our speaker today is well known to you," began the first gentleman on the podium. "He needs no introduction."

"I am the Great Oz," said the second speaker, and he obviously felt that explanation was enough.

"My paper is rather long and definitely learned, and I intend to stop for a great many sips of water while I am reading it," Dr. Oz explained and went on. "The title, as you already know, is 'On the Possibility That the Pied Piper Will Not Return.'"

"Oh, but he will! He promised!" cried Zane.

"Young lady, that will be quite enough," Dr. Oz said severely. "My observation is that you are entirely too young to be attending this lecture in the first place, and in the second place, I am quite certain that before too long the evidence will convince you that the Pied Piper as you know him is entirely fictional, or perhaps I should say mythological. The so-called historical evidence is fragmentary at best, and what there is suggests that a massive elaboration has occurred, whereby miraculous elements are grafted on to satisfy the needs of people who yearn for such elements in the stories they hear—but these have no basis in fact whatsoever."

"I rather liked the story the way it was," Lady Zane whispered to the others. "And I don't think my belief was especially connected to historical evidence."

The Cougar and the Cowpoke were entirely over their heads. The Piute was daydreaming. Dr. Oz droned on.

"Some scholars contend that there was a person who entered the town of Hamelin on the River Weser through the East Gate on the Feast of Saints John and Paul, on June 26, 1284, and beguiled a group of some 130 children—the number is variously reported—out of the town. Earliest records of this event are very sketchy. The date for the departure of the children is given as the same day, June 26. A window in the Market Church (circa 1300) depicts such an event with a Piper in multicolored attire surrounded by a group of children. Allusions are made in later diaries, especially those by Johannes Weier (1566) and Heinrich Bunting (1586). I quote directly from these works:

> A certain flute player was engaged to lure rats away from Hamelin. When his work was done, he received only abuse instead of his agreed reward and was displeased. In the year 1284, on June 26, one hundred and thirty children from Hamelin followed this piper, who was clad in multicolored clothes. They followed him to Calvary Mountain, where they were swallowed up. It was said that two children turned back, but one was mute and the other blind.

"It is worthy of remark," Dr. Oz continued, "that the mythologizing of these slender historical data had already fully advanced by the sixteenth century. But for the modern reader, no such mythologizing is to be desired. To the contrary, what is needed is a detached and dispassionate review of the data. Such a reading at once establishes clearly that the Piper, if he existed, was in no way connected to the removal of rats from the city. This is a mere folktale grafted onto the event for its spell-binding power with credulous medieval audiences.

"Instead, it is far more likely that the Pied Piper, if such a person must be regarded as historical, had been engaged by the townspeople to relieve the children's symptoms of Saint Anthony's Fire, a disease causing its victims to dance, a circumstance well documented by students of bizarre occurrences during the medieval period. I draw the reader's attention to well-documented material by the contemporary American writer John Fuller in his book *The Day of St. Anthony's Fire.*"

"Pardon me, sir . . . ah, Dr. Oz? Could you explain what the dancing disease actually is?" Lady Zane's voice rang out childlike and clear.

"By all means," Dr. Oz said graciously. "There was often in the Middle Ages a curious ailment brought on by the purple funqus ergot, which grows on rye bread in damp circumstances. A person who consumed the infected bread was likely to be afflicted with violent spasmodic cramps and mental aberrations. Technically, ergot poisoning follows this course: the blood vessels are constricted, which causes burning sensations in the hands and feet. Sometimes hallucinations occur. These hallucinations are not unlike those contemporary people experience after using the drug LSD (lysergic acid diethylamide), which happens to be an ergot derivative."

"Then you are saying that the Pied Piper story is true but different from what we're used to thinking?" asked Lady Zane.

"There is little doubt that the Piper must have existed. But to identify him as a savior figure leading the children into a mountainside of heavenly bliss is a gross misrepresentation. No doubt he did play a flute; no doubt the children danced in response to it. These events are entirely plausible, though we have no proof that they actually occurred. What is not plausible or believable is that the Pied Piper had magic powers—that the mountain opened when he played his pipe, that the children disappeared into the mountain.

"Most doubtful of all is the aspect of the child or children left behind, to whom the Piper promised to return. Here it is undeniable that the mythologers have been at work, confusing the Piper with a Christ figure, elaborating the myth in a way that is grossly misleading."

"What proof do you have that your version or account of these events is true?" Lady Zane wanted to know.

"Young lady, the word *proof* is no longer useful and smacks of an overdependency on the rational, an overinvolvement with the historicity of the account. Were we, merely for the sake of argument, to transpose the terms of our discussion to scriptural scholarship, I would have to say that you are attempting to return to the Piper level."

At this point, Dr. Oz began to smile, a giant smile that took over his face. What amused him was the wittiness of his own comparison, a joke that he proceeded at once to explain for listeners less learned than himself.

"I mean of course, the Piper level in the same sense that New Testament scholars would refer to the Jesus level, a level that, I may add, is entirely beyond us. Who the real Jesus may have been and who the real Piper may have been are entirely matters of conjecture."

"Of course," Lady Zane said quietly, understanding his meaning at last. She looked rather sadly at the Cougar, the Cowpoke and the Piute guide. The lecture had eluded them, and they were staring distractedly at the statues and decorations around the lecture room. Even Rover was snoozing peacefully, his sides heaving, a gentle snore being heard now and then from underneath Lady Zane's chair.

"But I suppose," Lady Zane went on, "I am free to go on believing? If it suits my fancy? If it doesn't contradict my experience?"

"It's foolhardy, of course. But on the other hand, you are entirely free to do so," said Dr. Oz.

"You see, Dr. Oz, the shape of the story is just right. It matches my best understanding of reality. The town of Hamelin, the plague, the trickery of the town fathers, the trust of the children, the silver flute, the multicolored clothes—everything seems to ring true, as if it were the Gospel truth."

The Piute, who had begun listening after all, said, "Don't forget, Zane, how the Piper fits in with the Gospel itself:

We piped you a tune, but you would not dance!
We played dirges, but you wouldn't be mourners!

"Something tells me the story is true," Lady Zane said firmly. "In a very deep way I could never explain, in my bones I am sure the Pied Piper will come back, just as he said he would. For the lame child and the mute child who were left, wishing and yearning for their time of bliss.

"Do you understand, Dr. Oz?" Zane continued. "We are the ones who have been left behind. We are the children waiting. The Piper is coming for us, and we have only to wait patiently, in faith, and he will return just as he said."

"But, young woman, if the Piper made that promise, it was in approximately the year 1284, perhaps as late as 1300, and we are still waiting," noted Dr. Oz.

"Ah yes, but this is mythic time," said Lady Zane. "Our patience and his response. Our waiting and yearning and his passionate pursuit of us, all this is happening now while we are sitting and standing here. So even though it seems we are waiting, we are also not waiting at all, because the Kingdom is here and now. Even though the Piper has not returned, it has already happened that he has chosen us. So our waiting is not in vain."

"You are an impossible child," snapped Dr. Oz. "You will not listen to reason. I have presented an airtight case, open and shut, to prove that the Pied Piper is highly unlikely to return, if indeed he ever existed at all."

"And I have decided to believe in him anyway. Dr. Oz, the next thing I know you will be trying to say is there isn't any God," Lady Zane countered.

"There is no sense letting children into lecture halls. They invariably ask infuriating questions and divert the audience from a consideration of legitimate scholarly concerns," Dr. Oz harumphed.

Then a learned woman in another part of the audience stood up and said, "I am concerned, Dr. Oz, about the adverse psychological effects of this story on the children to whom it is being told. And I would like to suggest that you see to it that the laws of the land are altered in such a way that stories of this nature, with untold psychological impact, cannot be inflicted on innocent children, and thus cause deep emotional scars."

"Madam," Dr. Oz protested, holding up his hands in a mock gesture of self-defense, "I have no such power to change the laws of the land."

But Lady Zane said, "Please, the story has a wisdom in it that must not be changed. It is more profound than we can tell; we must go on telling it. If it frightens us, that is only because we are afraid of wisdom and truth."

"But you yourself are a child, you can't possibly decide," the learned woman protested.

But Lady Zane and her companions had lost interest in the words of the learned lady and the erudite Dr. Oz. Now they could hear the sound of a silver flute piping, and the figure of the Piper in his ragged clothes was crystal clear.

Dr. Oz had no notion of the Piper's presence. And when Lady Zane and the others began to dance, with vigorous, jerky, spontaneous motions, Dr. Oz became embarrassed and distraught. He thought they undoubtedly were insulting or humiliating him. But Lady Zane and the other adventurers had completely forgotten Dr. Oz and his scholarly learning. They were spellbound and enchanted listening to the unearthly music, and they saw the Piper clearly, leading them a merry chase.

CHAPTER FIFTEEN

Breathing a Thinner Air

———————————

In which the Impossible Child
and her companions get
where they're going at last.

Wasn't it a funny dream! Perfectly bewilderin'!
Last night, and night before, and night before that,
Seemed like I saw the march of regiments o' children
Marching to the robin's fife and cricket's rat-ta-tat!
Lily-banners overhead, with the dew upon 'em,
On flashed the little army, as with sword and flame;
Like the buzz o' bumble-wings, with the honey on
'em,
Came an eerie, cheery chant, chiming as it came:—

Where go the children? Traveling! Traveling!
Where go the children, travelling ahead?
Some go to kindergarten; some go to day-school;
Some go to night-school; and some go to bed!

Smooth roads or rough roads, warm or winter
weather,
On go the children, tow-head and brown,
Brave boys and brave girls, rank and file together,

Marching out of Morning-Land, over dale and
down;
Some go a-gypsying out in country places—
Out through the orchards, with blossoms on the
boughs
Wild, sweet and pink and white as their own glad
faces;
And some go, at evening, calling home the cows.

T hen the pilgrim children found themselves breathing a thinner air. They had
come near the top of Calvary Mountain, and the
figure on the path ahead of them seemed to vanish
from sight.

Even so, they followed him faithfully. All at
once, in the curve of the mountain path they saw
a lady with a book in her hand, and around her
head was a circle of stars, which glittered like royal
diamonds. The lady was beautiful; she took their
breath away.

"These are the times of the great mercy," she
said. "These are the times of the triumph. Do not
become discouraged by the difficulties you find before you.

"These are the times of the great return. When
all those who are among the chosen will be gath-
ered in—the weakest, the littlest, the most fragile,
those who have suffered most, those who are fur-

thest away and lost—all will come, all will come together, all will come in.

"And the air and the breath of this new creation
will be like the breathing of the love of the Father
who rules over us all, with an inexhaustible love.
And Jesus will reign."

So they stood there in the clear mountain air
until the vision faded. And they knew they had
seen what they had seen.

Their innocence had been given back to them,
and the weary soil of centuries was being taken
away. The burden of their sins and offenses was
slipping from their shoulders, and they skipped up
the mountain path like goats. It was easy to run
and jump and play.

They ran, they scampered, and they sang, even
though they knew what mountain it was. At last
they were not afraid of Calvary.

Somewhere near the top it would be their priv-
ilege to be crucified. The nails would be driven into
their hands, and they would pass over and
through.

They knew it could be painful, but it would be
their redemption, their vindication, their consolation. And they ran to it like scampering mountain
dwellers, sure footed, without fear.

There was a stillness around them, a hush of
awe and a rush of transcendence they could never
describe or explain. They knew the Lord was with

them, in the midst of them, leading them on. They were no longer sure where the line was drawn between the living and the dead.

Then they saw the holy city descending, dressed like a bride, beautiful, radiant, and the Lord reached out for her with both hands, as his beloved. And the union of earth and heaven was consummated as a passionate entering in. And there was no night there.

"What place is this? Where are we now? When did we pass from walking on the mountain to walking into it?" they asked in wonder.

But they were all thinking the same question. "Are we there? Where we are destined for, where we are meant to be?"

They had moved into a different mode of existence, a new place not possible before.

They saw then the light filtering through an early morning mist, and they heard fiddles tuning.

The sign was straight ahead, reading:

> RESURRECTION CITY
> FELICIANA PARISH
> Population 144,000
> Incorporated circa A.D. 33
> Home of the Saints
> WELCOME HOME,
> EXPEDITION OF LADY ZANE
> AND FRIENDS

It was clear that the best and most royal mode of entry to the town was by way of a river raft, and Lady Zane summoned her Companions on board. Dreamily they poled and drifted. Time was of no consequence.

As the current carried them along, they saw profusions of flowers: wisterias and magnolias, azalea and oleander, blooming regardless of season. Then Zane spied a mother pelican with her head turned to the left, and seeming to open her breast to feed her young.

Then they caught sight of Cousin Brandon, sitting on his front gallery, reading a newspaper called *The True Democrat*. He rocked gently back and forth in his rocking chair, surveying the breadth of the river as the children poled their raft in to the bank.

Cousin Brandon's house was on high ground, too high for alligators and water moccasins to get in. It was too high for marsh or swamp, but there were sounds of frogs and crickets joining in an insect concerto, and now and then a bobwhite let out a piercing cry.

"You mean to tell us, Cousin Brandon, heaven isn't any more than what some writers told us? Just from using their imagination? No more than that?" said Zane in wonder.

"You know yourself, Zane. High time you stopped your fooling and looked reality straight in the eye. You know as much about this damn fool

revelation as I do. Pure invention. Now, this Kingdom you've been chasing? You knew all about it in
your heart of hearts. You're home at last, you and
your fellow travelers. What's more, you didn't have
to go anywhere to get here."

"Don't think you can rattle us, Cousin, with all
your cynical talk," said Zane. "We know you have
the faith just as we do."

Cousin Brandon shook his head reflectively.
He'd known the Zanes and the Storeys for generations. They'd always had a fanciful streak.

"Don't you recall what I told you, that Feliciana
Parish is an enclave and that only a few will get
in?" And Brandon grinned from ear to ear.

Zane thought he must be right. In the church-
yard beyond the gate, she could see all the family
monuments; and everywhere, Feliciana flowers
were in bloom.

The gate was twisted nearly off its hinges, but
the pilgrims found a way to swing it open. As they
began to leave, Cousin Brandon made them stretch
out their hands, and he gave them what Louisiana
people call lagniappe—that is, a little something
unexpected, a surprise. It was about the size of a
small wrapped candy, but on inspection, the travelers saw it was really a little white stone to tell
them their right names.

Then they were filled with knowledge. They
knew as much as any human being could know.

They knew the dead were raised, though they hadn't quite seen them yet. But when they walked among the gravestones, they knew the blessed ones would be there, visiting and smiling and passing the time of day.

Now the music seemed closer. They could hear the tap and shuffle of dancing down the way at the American Legion Hall. The caller's voice was chanting out: "Allemande left on your left hand, right to your partner and a right and left grand."

"Who's that dancing, Brandon?" asked Zane.

"Oh, I expect those are the inmates from Angola State Prison that were lately set free."

The gate swung easily on its hinges. The pilgrims tried riding the gate back and forth a couple of times before going through.

"Guess I never thought it would be like Louisiana," Lady Zane said.

She skipped down the street, holding the white stone in her hand. There was still plenty of time to read it, no sense rushing things. She knew she had all the time in the world.

Then came another sound—a railroad train puffing into Feliciana Station. And Lady Zane passed by the general store where Aunt Jo and Uncle Ulloa almost starved to death trying to be storekeepers when they had no heart for it. Down by the river they could hear a calliope pumping, a riverboat pulling in, surely.

And over near the middle of town, that was the best of all—a political rally, sure as anything. But there wasn't any shouting or fighting. Instead everybody was harmonizing like a barbershop quartet. They could barely make the words out at first, but then they came through stronger and sharper. Sure enough, it was Governor Huey Long's campaign song, the one he had half written himself. It was based on the idea that everyone would be a king, but this time it wasn't just a glossy political promise. They knew for sure they were in the place of justice, where every tear had been wiped away, and that there was no more death. And everyone had to admit that the Lord had a pretty good imagination. It had to be the end all and be all when even Huey Long, of all people, came out looking like a kingfish, a prophet, and a priest.

Why weep and slumber, America,
Land of brave and true
There are castles and clothing enough to share
All belongs to you.
Every man a king, every man a king,
Oh, you can be a millionaire,
As long as there's something for others,
There's enough for all people to share,

When it's sunny June or December too,
Or in the wintertime or spring,

There'll be peace without end
Every neighbor a friend,
And every man a king.

Notes

ix *The Kingdom goes before us:* author's own verse.

4   *"What description":* Matthew 11:17, 24, *The Jerusalem Bible* (TJB).

17 *"Holy Michael Archangel":* traditional prayer.

17 *"He shall give":* Psalm 91: 11–12, King James Version (KJV), paraphrased.

18–19 *Michael before God shining,* author's own verse

21–22 *Shall I go with you,* author's own verse.

24–25 *"But to this":* from chapter 68, *The Cloud of Unknowing,* edited by William Johnston (New York: Doubleday Image Books, 1973), page 136.

26 *It is like that expression of Whitehead's,* see Alfred North Whitehead, *Process and Reality,* (New York: Macmillan Publishing Co., 1929) page 41 and throughout.

26 *"See, I am":* Isaiah 43:19, TJB.

26–27 *"The wolf lives":* Isaiah, 11:6–9, TJB.

30–31 *"Where the bee":* William Shakespeare, *The Tempest,* 5.1.88-94.

32 *James Dickey's poem:* see *James Dickey Poems 1957–1967,* (Middletown, Conn: Wesleyan University Press, 1967.) The poem, "Falling," is a lyrical meditation on existence and death, based on a factual account of an airline stewardess who was sucked from an airplane and fell to her death from a great height.

35–36 *"Prayer is the":* Emily Dickinson, *Selected Poems and Letters* (New York: Doubleday Anchor Books, 1959), page 121.

38–39 *"I advise you":* Lewis Carroll, *Alice in Wonderland,* chapter 1, as it appears in *The Annotated Alice,* with Introduction and Notes by Martin Gardner (New York: Clarkson N. Potter, Inc., 1960), pages 32–33.

39 *"What wert thou":* ibid., page 26.

42 *"My mind to me":* Edward Dyer, "Another of the Same—Excellently Written by a Most Woorthy [sic] Gentleman" as it appears in *Sixteenth-Century English Poetry,* edited by Norman E. McClure (New York: Harper & Brothers, 1954), page 205; the sixteenth-century spelling has been modernized by the author.

43   *"And Mary said;"* Luke 1:46–47, 49, KJV.

44–45   *What, then, are we . . .* author's own prose poem.

47–48   *"Mine is a long":* Lewis Carroll, *Alice in Wonderland,* pages chapter 3, 50–51.

52–53   *"In a house . . . cease to love":* from the lyrics to a traditional Mardi Gras song.

59   *"When the businessman":* G. K. Chesterton, "The Ethics of Elfland," Chapter 4, *Orthodoxy,* as it appears in *G. K. Chesterton: Collected Works,* vol. 1 (San Francisco: Ignatius Press, 1986), page 249.

60–61   *1 Corinthians 7:29–31, Revised Standard Version (RSV).*

65–66   *"The publicly owned corporation . . . reorganize local government":* Edward G. Harness, "Views on Corporate Responsibility." Pamphlet (Cincinnati, OH: The Procter & Gamble Company, 1977), pages 4–14.

71–72   *"Take heed lest":* Deuteronomy 8:11–20, RSV.

83   *"Blow, wind, blow!":* a traditional nursery rhyme.

85–86   *"Into the street . . . salt is sprinkled":* Robert Browning, "The Pied Piper of Hamelin: A Child's Story," stanzas 7 and 12, as it appears in *Poems of Robert Browning,* edited by Humphrey Milford (London: Oxford University Press, 1949), pages 230, 232–33.

89–90   *"And when all":* ibid., stanza 3, pages 233–34.

91   *Maurice Maeterlinck's fairy tale:* see *The Blue Bird: A Fairy Play in Six Acts,* translated by Alexander Teixeira de Mattos (New York: Dodd, Mead and Company, 1913).

91   *"How do you":* "The Swing," Robert Louis Stevenson, *A Child's Garden of Verses* (New York: Random House, 1978), page 12.

93   *"Happiness":* all of the Happinesses listed here are characters in Maeterlinck's play, *The Blue Bird.*

94   The Great Joys are also characters in *The Blue Bird.*

95   *"Happy are the Poor":* author's paraphrase of Matthew 5:3–11, TJB.

96   *"And God shall":* author's paraphrase of Revelation 21:4, TJB.

98   *"I am the Great Oz":* the Oz in this context is not the wizard in Frank L. Baum's works, but rather a learned person of the author's invention.

100   *"A certain flute":* Gloria Skurzynski, *What Happened in Hamelin* (New York: Four Winds Press, 1979).

104   *"We piped you":* author's paraphrase of Matthew, 11:17, KJV.

107–8   *"Wasn't it a funny":* James Whitcomb Riley, "Dream-March," in *The Book of Joyous Children* (Freeport, NY: Books for Libraries Press, 1969 reprint of 1902 edition), pages 10–12, *passim.*

114–15   *"Why weep and slumber":* lyrics from "Every Man a King," words and music by Huey P. Long, and Castro Carazo (New Orleans, LA: National Book Co., 1935); sheet music found in the Lower Mississippi Valley Collections, Louisiana State University Libraries, Baton Rouge, LA.